JESSE JACKSON

BY EDDIE STONE

An Original Holloway House Edition

HOLLOWAY HOUSE PUBLISHING CO.
LOS ANGELES, CALIFORNIA

Published by
HOLLOWAY HOUSE PUBLISHING COMPANY
8060 Melrose Avenue, Los Angeles, CA 90046
Any similarity to persons living or dead is purely coincidental.
International Standard Book Number 0-87067-840-X
Printed in the United States of America
Cover photograph by Jeffery
Cover design by Jeff Renfro

All inside photos by Jeffery

CONTENTS

Introduction

Not since the heydays of the Civil Rights Movement of the late '50s and '60s has America, or the world for that matter, been exposed to an orator of the caliber of the Reverend Jesse Louis Jackson, country preacher and politician, but not necessarily in that order.

In many respects the public life of Jesse Jackson began with the assassination of Dr. Martin Luther King, Jr. on April 4, 1968. From that moment in time, when Jackson stepped from the shadow of the older, veteran leadership of the movement, to the late '80s, Jackson has become the most well-known black leader since King.

The agony of King's death staggered and stagnated the Civil Rights Movement, and while Jackson, alone, is not to be credited for the advances made in the arena of Civil

Rights over the past 20 years, he has singularly been responsible for keeping the plight of "forgotten and voiceless" Americans—blacks, the poor, women, etc., before the national and world court through his ability to draw media attention to himself and therefore any cause he might espouse.

What Jackson has proven over the past 20 years is the power of the media in this country and his power over that very powerful force. The national press was there when Jackson declared himself a candidate for the Democratic Presidential nomination in 1983, saying "Mindful of the urgency of our times, I stand before you to acknowledge that, after deep reflection, the voice had duty has whispered, 'Thou must.' I rise to declare that 'I can.' "

Skeptics and critics scampered from the political woodworks to decry Jackson's campaign as the "impossible dream." A dream that might well have a nighmarish backlash against those people about the business of removing Ronald Reagan from office, a great deal more important than a "symbolic campaign" staged by a black candidate.

But there were believers. Enough to stoke the boilers on Jackson's "freedom train," with Jackson heralding, from coast-to-coast, "Get on board! Get on board! But you got to be registered to ride!"

The Jackson "odyssey" had officially begun, though there are any number of people who believe that Jesse Jackson was on a course he had set as a child, fulfilling the promise made to all Americans—that any one of them could aspire to the highest office in the land.

There were any number of hazards along the way—an

offensive aside that split Jackson from one of blacks' traditional allies, Jews; his association with the controversial Black Muslim leader Louis Farrakhan; a lack of meaningful support from noted black leaders who saw the Jackson candidacy as something less than "real politics," and a "symbolic political effort which will reap some symbolic benefits."

It didn't matter. Few knew, or could believe that this urbanized "country preacher" had a plan, not simply for black people but for the country, realized in the formation of Jackson's Rainbow Coalition.

"The resolution of the race question in this country would liberate others around the world," said Jackson. "For until white America is what it ought to be, black America cannot be what it ought to be. And until black Americans are no longer prohibited by race from achieving their potential, all Americans will be poorer as a result."

Jackson offered a possibility that few, if any blacks had ever given any serious thought to. Unlike the token campaigns of militants like Eldridge Cleaver, Jackson's appeal was in that he believed he could be president, and he was transferring that belief, that strong faith to others. "We can move from the slave ship to the championship!" said Jackson, and people listened. "From the guttermost to the uppermost! From the outhouse to the courthouse! From the statehouse to the White House!"

The Jackson Campaign '84 and the more successful Campaign '88 have written Jackson into American history books in large letters. But it would be wrong to point to these major events as the sum total of Jackson's success.

Dr. Martin Luther King, Jr. once said, "The racial problem will be solved in America to the degree every American considers himself personally confronted with it."

Jackson brought the problems and aspirations into the corporate board rooms of America and gained an audience denied others, no less sincere.

The ecstasy of the Jesse Jackson years came on July 17, 1984 as he stood before the Democratic National Convention in San Francisco and, representing the diverse membership of the Rainbow Coalition, delivered the speech that will be remembered and committed to memory by school children along with King's historic "I Have A Dream Speech."

Jackson will long be remembered for bringing the political congregation to its feet with: "Suffering breeds character. Character breeds faith. And in the end, faith will not disappoint. Faith, hope and dreams will prevail. We must be bound together by faith sustained by hope and driven by a dream. Troubles won't last always. Our time has come. Our time has come. Our time has come!"

Chapter 1

The Changing of the Guard

The omens were bad that spring in Memphis, Tennessee. The large Southern town had yet to see a civil rights demonstration, and none of its population had gone through the traumatic changes which had befallen a Birmingham or a Selma. Memphis, in union jargon, was a "closed town."

In March of 1968, however, two garbage workers were killed in a freak accident, and the doors to civil protest were opened. The incident occurred at the city's main garage, where a driving rain had postponed work and maintenance on the trucks. The mechanics and workers had sought shelter inside the foreman's shack. They were white men and thought nothing of ducking in out of the rain.

But when two black workers tried to seek the same shelter, they were told to leave. "No niggers in here," was the word. The two blacks left and went outside, trying to get into the cabs of the garbage trucks. But the doors were locked. In desperation, they crouched into the truck bins, lit cigarettes and settled in to wait out the downpour.

A short in the electrical system of the truck in which they were sitting caused the bin mechanism to begin working. The two black workers were trapped, crushed amidst a pile of garbage as they were raised into the main holding tank and dumped.

Word spread of the tragic deaths to the local organizers and ministers affiliated with the Southern Christian Leadership Conference. A protest march was organized on the local levels in support of the black garbage workers who went on strike to protest the needless deaths, and local leaders decided to go for broke. They contacted Dr. Martin Luther King, Jr., and asked him to join them in Memphis.

Dr. Ralph Abernathy and Andy Young, Dr. King's two highest ranking lieutenants within the SCLC, pleaded with their leader not to go to Memphis. The SCLC had already begun working on the upcoming poor people's march, scheduled to take place in April of that year. The task was a tremendous one, and both Abernathy and Young felt that King did not have the time, nor the energy, to march with blacks in Memphis.

Martin Luther King, known to his staff as "Doc," was a man who moved to the calling of his own mind. Only recently, and against all advice from his staff and other black leaders throughout the country, King had publicly come out against the war in Vietnam. King had known what the consequences of such a position would be. Lyndon Johnson, considered by many the best friend the black man ever had, was quickly succumbing to the powerful wave of anti-war sentiment in the country. By having King protest the war, Johnson would lose even more face amongst his constituency. He would also react adversely, cutting off funds for projects which had been developed over the last ten years. But King was not to be morally blackmailed by economic issues. His sense of right and his sense of justice forced him to throw caution to the wind and take a stand.

With his schedule already jammed with speeches, meetings and the huge project of gathering together hundreds of thousands of the nation's poor and marching them into the Capitol, Dr. King agreed to go to Memphis and help with the strikers and demonstrators.

On March 28, 1968, Martin Luther King came to Memphis to lead a march through the downtown sector in support of the striking sanitation workers. What occurred that day was an omen of the violence that would shock the world within a week.

As the marchers came to an intersection near the center of town, shoving began in the front lines. Two black youths, marching with King, began pushing King as though trying to protect him from some unknown assailant. King stumbled and almost fell. Andy Young grabbed his arm and pulled him from the crowd. With his aides guarding him, King was rushed to a waiting limousine and sped away.

The momentary confusion and outbreak of shoving had caused the police to move. The crowd, boxed into the street, began fighting back. A riot ensued, one that left a protester dead, sixty people injured and over 400 arrested.

Back at his hotel, King was furious. He felt that the riot had been started unnecessarily. He was angry with those staff members who had not shown up in Memphis, arguing that the Poor People's March was of greater importance. King's anger lasted, and two days later, he berated his entire staff for not following orders and leaving the movement weak. Among those King screamed at was the Reverend Jesse Jackson, the flamboyant and young organizer, head of King's Operation Breadbasket in Chicago. Young Jesse Jackson took his punishment and scolding along with everyone else.

The seeds of violence had been sown in Memphis, and now King's aides pleaded with him to leave the city. There existed within the Southern town an undercurrent of impending doom. The National Guard lined the streets, armed with live weapons. The police patrolled the sidewalks. And the local newspapers were after King to leave.

An investigation into the riot itself turned up information which was to shock and frighten King's men. The two black youths who had pushed King during the march confessed to being paid off by the FBI to instigate trouble. It occurred to many of King's aides that not only were they being watched and harassed by the FBI from the outside, but that their arch enemy, J. Edgar Hoover, had also managed to infiltrate their organization from within.

Memphis seemed a dangerous place, a city that would

not let go—a city quietly plotting against the movement and the men who led it. King had seen danger before, and had felt fear, but he was determined to stay, to see the garbage strike through and help his oppressed brothers. The younger aides on the staff were adamantly opposed to staying in Memphis, but King was their leader and his voice remained strong.

The following days in Memphis helped to soothe the rifts which had risen within the organization. Once the decision had been made to stay, everyone pitched in and began working towards a common goal. Ralph Abernathy, Andy Young, Jesse Jackson and King's usual entourage of aides gathered together at the Lorraine Motel, a black owned business, and began making preparations for a huge rally in downtown Memphis.

On April 3, King addressed a cheering crowd at a local Baptist Church. His last speech was an oration which has gone down in the history books as possibly one of the finest ever given. King spoke eloquently about his own death, telling his adoring listeners that he "had been to the mountaintop." In retrospect, the speech was eerie in that the great black leader seemed to be mystically in touch with the events that would lead to his death the following evening at the Lorraine Motel.

The speech over, King returned to room 306 at the Lorraine Motel. The following day, the 4th, would be spent working with aides on the Poor People's March and organizing strategy for the Memphis project. That night, King and his staff were due for dinner at the home of the Reverend Samuel Kyles, pastor of Monumental Baptist Church in Memphis.

It was at this dinner that King hoped to bring his staff together after their chaotic and divisive week in Memphis. The anger which King had felt towards his aides had disappeared, but there still lingered much tension between himself and his loyal aides.

The greatest rift had arisen between King and Jesse Jackson. Jackson, flying between Atlanta, Chicago and Memphis, had questioned King hard on the Poor People's campaign. Jackson found it difficult to believe that the march on Washington D.C. could work. In his mind, bringing that many of the nation's poor together would take a miracle, and besides, Jackson was concerned over what would happen once the masses were huddled together beneath the Capitol dome.

Staying on King's heels, seeking answers to his questions, Jackson discovered himself the object of the Doctor's fury. At one point, King had turned and snapped at Jackson, telling the young, audacious man to go out and find his own niche in society, and to just leave him (King) alone. Most of the staff had heard King, and most likely there existed a hidden sense of pleasure among them at seeing the young Reverend being handled that way.

Jesse Jackson had risen through the ranks of the SCLC quickly. He was an attention getter. Handsome, eloquent and brilliant, many of the staff members had come to resent his ability to grab headlines and get his picture into the newspapers. Only a day before the scheduled dinner with the Reverend Kyles, Jackson had managed to leap into a photo-shooting session involving King and Abernathy. Jesse appeared prominently in the photographs, and his face appeared on the front pages of newspapers throughout the country.

There were men on King's staff who felt that the publicity accorded Jesse Jackson was unfair; that there were others who had worked harder, from the beginning, who should have been receiving the attention. But there seemed to be no stopping this young man who had begun to capture the imagination of the country's blacks. Jesse Jackson was a ''comer,'' and everyone seemed to sense it.

The brief pleasure which some might have felt when King turned on Jackson was short lived. King went out of his way to invite Jackson to dinner with Reverend Kyles, a gesture that allowed King to open the doors and allow Jackson back into the fold.

At about a quarter to six on that fateful evening of April 4, King and his staff were preparing to leave for dinner. Jesse Jackson was dressed casually, in a sweater and slacks. Jackson was usually the butt of many jibes from the staff for his casual attitude towards dress. Whereas King and his men made it a point to dress in a suit and tie, the young Jackson opted for the styles of the younger generation. In a way, Jesse was telling them that the old guard was passing, and that he was the epitome of the new power.

The kidding over Jackson's dress continued as the men prepared to leave for dinner. Jackson stood downstairs with Andy Young, King's chief lieutenant, King's attorney Chauncy Eskridge, and King's personal secretary James Bevel. King emerged onto the balcony and began chatting with his men below. Jackson introduced a saxophone player named Ben Branch, and King delighted the musician by requesting that he play ''Precious Lord'' later that night at a gathering.

Solomon Jones, King's driver, then told King that he felt a chill in the air, and advised King to don a coat. King replied that he would. Reverend Kyles, leaving the second floor balcony at the Lorraine Motel, told King over his shoulder that he would take some of the party with him, since there were more coming to dinner than had first been expected.

The time was 6:01 P.M. The date, April 4, 1968.

The town of Memphis was quiet. On the balcony and in the courtyard below, a group of highly educated, powerful black men joked and bantered back and forth. On the second floor balcony, the most powerful and righteous leader of black men this country had ever known awaited a bullet.

The gunshot sounded to the aides like a car back-firing. The chill in the April evening had turned to frost. Martin Luther King, Jr., lay sprawled on the balcony in front of room 306, blood spurting from a deep wound in his neck.

The first man to arrive at his side was Ralph Abernathy, who cradled King in his arms and patted his cheek. Later, Abernathy would tell the press that King had looked at him with fear in his eyes and with a silent message for Abernathy to carry on. In fact, Abernathy had been the stated heir to the SCLC leadership. Only days after the assassination of President John Kennedy, King had named his vice-president and executive director president of the SCLC in the event of his death. It was only right that the next in command should hold the dying leader to his chest.

Pandemonium broke out at the Lorraine Motel. King's

aides ran to the second floor and surrounded their fallen leader. Someone tried to call an ambulance, but the switchboard operator, a black woman, had died of a heart attack the moment the shot was fired. As the men searched and screamed for a phone, the police arrived, along with an ambulance. The officers asked where the shot had been fired from, and the aides pointed across the street toward the fire department building. The police began searching.

The ambulance attendants began lifting King onto the stretcher. But Abernathy, Young and a few other aides insisted on moving the body themselves. A towel had been placed against King's wound in a vain attempt to stop the blood flow. That crimson soaked cloth fell to the ground as King was lifted onto the stretcher.

Jesse Jackson yelled and tried to help as much as the next man that evening, but there was nothing anyone could do. Stunned, horrified and realizing the tragedy which had befallen them, the aides moved aimlessly in and out of the rooms at the Lorraine Motel as they watched the ambulance turn around in the courtyard below and drive off to the hospital.

Jackson walked into a room and finally got an outside line. He put in a call to King's wife, Coretta, and told her that she had better come to Memphis. No one yet knew if King would survive.

At the hospital, they lost Martin Luther King. Andy Young insisted on witnessing the autopsy, a precaution against losing the initial reports as had been the case with John Kennedy's autopsy.

The nation sat stunned for the second time in less than a decade in front of their television sets as news of King's death interrupted every program on the air. Little was known at the time beyond the fact that the great black leader had been slain by an assassin's bullet at the Lorraine Motel in Memphis. Almost two months later to the day, the nation would sit again in stunned silence as news of Robert Kennedy's death in Los Angeles interrupted regular programming.

By 6:30 that evening, less than a half hour after the shot had been fired, the camera crews from the three networks began arriving. NBC, CBS, and ABC began filming and attempting to get interviews. It was agreed within the circle of King's men that no one should talk with the press, at least not at this time, but according to sources who were there, Jesse Jackson began speaking with the newsmen, telling them that he was the last person Martin Luther King, Jr., had spoken with.

To many of the men standing around that night in a shocked stupor, this action on the part of Jesse Jackson was incomprehensible. It was nothing less than the beginning of a controversy that would eventually split the SCLC wide open, and allow Jackson to emerge as the one spokesman for the black man in America. At the time, King's aides could not believe what they were witnessing. Ralph Abernathy would later claim that Jackson could not have said that he was the last person to be with King, because Abernathy himself was. Conflicting stories would circulate as to where Jesse Jackson was standing, and what he was doing at the moment the shots were fired.

It is evident now, some twenty years after the fact, that Jesse Jackson, either by fact or fiction, managed to emerge that evening as the spokesman for the movement. While

Abernathy remained silent, shaken to the roots, Jesse Jackson talked to the press. Whether his intent was manipulative or instinctual, Jackson had taken the reins.

As a nation of angered blacks and sorrowful whites looked on, Jesse Jackson appeared on their television screens. The networks carried his words and focused their cameras on him. The effect was the same as when Lyndon Johnson stepped forward at Love Field in Dallas that Friday night in 1963 and assured the American people that the transfer of power had taken place. For hours, 180 million people were not even sure if their government existed. Lyndon Johnson allowed the nation, even the world, to mourn without restraint, to shed tears without fear. He had stepped forward and taken leadership.

For the millions of blacks who had known no other leader than Martin Luther King, there was a void. It was a terrific, dark hole where once there had been a shining light. As opposed to the Kennedy-Johnson transfer of power, there was no Constitution that could be used to insure millions of people the security of an orderly transfer of power. King had been a spiritual leader, as well as a political leader of men. It was understood that no man could ever duplicate his greatness. But on that night of April 4, the black population of America needed one man who would step forward and promise to carry the torch.

Ralph Abernathy was that man. At least, King had personally chosen him to be that man in the event of his death. But Ralph Abernathy did not step forward and speak. He did not restrain himself, bury his emotions and assume the position of a new leader upon whose shoulders fate had leveled an ominous burden. The nation, in 1963, had forgiven Lyndon Johnson his stuttering, difficult speech. They knew and respected his burden, and were thankful that he was trying. The nation of blacks would have done the same for Abernathy, had he merely elected to speak. But he didn't.

Instead, there was Jesse Jackson—dressed still in his casual sweater and slacks, a young man, handsome and with a beautiful speaking voice, a man whom some equated to King himself in his ability to elevate an audience to the heights of spiritual frenzy and purpose. As Jesse Jackson spoke to the newsmen, the staff of the SCLC stayed inside their motel rooms, still stunned by the loss of their beloved leader.

Jackson's action that evening has been condemned by many people in and outside the movement. "An opportunistic of the most cynical kind" the critics said in opposition of Jackson. In his defense, however, there are an equal number of supporters who present the argument stated above that the black nation was at the moment leaderless. A spokesman should have spoken. Ralph Abernathy should have seized the reins and spoken to the people of America, encouraging calm and a renewed commitment. As Lyndon Johnson had settled the American people into a weekend of mourning, so should have Abernathy quelled the unspoken fears and hatred that gripped the hearts of blacks and whites throughout America.

The greatest fears of those who abided by Martin Luther King's call for nonviolence were realized later that night. The blacks in America, who had been rising in larger and more active numbers against nonviolence, took their torches to their cities. Race riots occurred in one form or another throughout the country, with most major urban areas with high concentration of blacks erupting into infernos of violence and bloodshed. And still, the black leadership remained silent. All except for Jackson.

As the cities burned, and funeral arrangements were being made for King in Memphis, Jackson left the stricken city via airplane and headed for Chicago. The other members of the staff elected to stay with their leader's body in the South. Only Jackson opened himself to the wrath of the others and left.

The aides sat in the Lorraine Motel that night and prepared for King's funeral. Abernathy had given permission to Jackson to leave on the grounds that Jackson was going to Chicago to organize a planeload of blacks to fly down for the funeral. But Jesse Jackson obviously had other ideas.

As Jackson's airplane touched down at O'Hare Field, Chicago, like many other cities in the U.S., was burning. The blacks on the Southside had erupted. They were rampaging on the streets, burning, looting and destroying black and white businesses alike as they vented their rage. The riots were horrendous. Reports flooded out of Chicago that kids seven and eight years of age were looting and smashing windows. Fires destroyed more than ten million dollars worth of property. Over one thousand people were left homeless—all of them blacks.

Mayor Richard Daley, surveying the scene from a helicopter, issued an order to his police to "shoot to kill" anyone brandishing a weapon or a Molotov cocktail. In his order, Daley called arson the "worst and most hideous" of crimes. At the time, he made no mention of the fact that the greatest leader for non-violent struggle for freedom and justice had been slain by an assassin's bullet. Daley inflamed many by equating the burning of a liquor store with the murder of one of the greatest leaders in history. But Chicago was Daley's town, always had been and always would be.

Jesse Jackson landed in Chicago and immediately began pleading for order. At six o'clock that morning, twelve hours after the shot had been fired in Memphis, he appeared on the *Today Show* on the NBC network.

In Memphis, Abernathy, Young and the rest of King's staff watched with incredulous anger as Jesse Jackson sat in the NBC studios wearing the same sweater and slacks he had worn the evening before. The only difference was that the sweater was soaked with blood—the blood of Martin Luther King.

King's people claim that Jackson had taken the towel which had been used to stop the flow from King's wound and smeared the blood on his sweater. A media stunt was how some called it. Others were too infuriated to comment. But as they sat in their motel room in Memphis, Jesse Jackson once again went on national television and spoke about the tragedy and the future of the movement.

Later, Jesse Jackson addressed a special memorial session of the Chicago City Council, called for by Mayor Daley, obviously in an attempt to quell the riots which were destroying his city. Jackson appeared at the City Council Chambers with his blood-smeared sweater and spoke. "I am calling for nonviolence," he began, "in the homes, on the streets, in the classrooms, and in our relationships with one another. I'm challenging the youth today to be nonviolent as the greatest expression of faith they can make in Dr. King—to put your rocks down, put your bottles down.''

Mayor Daley made every effort to honor the man he had literally thrown out of Chicago only a short time before. Special sessions of the City Council had been called only twice before: once to honor President Kennedy, and once to honor Dan Ryan. Daley also proposed that a monument to Dr. King be erected. That monument later became Dr. Martin Luther King, Jr., Drive, a hundred blocks which ran through black neighborhoods in Chicago. The resolution, which passed the council with not one dissention, read:

''Whereas Dr. King possessed a deep and abiding conviction that when Americans were confronted with the contradiction between their cherished ideals of brotherhood in the religious sphere and the existence of hatred and racism, they would choose their ideal. And when confronted with the contradiction between their ideals of freedom and justice for all in the political sphere and the existence of poverty and prejudice, they would be faithful to their ideal.''

As Jesse Jackson sat in the City Council chambers, gazing at the huge portrait of King which adorned the far wall, he listened with growing bitterness to the resolution. A short time ago King had come to Chicago attempting to get fair housing for the Westside and Southside blacks and had been literally threatened by Daley and his machine. Reportedly, Daley, after listening to King turn down a compromise proposal to guarantee reasonable housing for the poor, had reminded the doctor that Chicago had been home to Al Capone. The inference was obvious.

But King was dead, and Daley was determined to honor him. Jackson listened as the resolution contained with a lofty tone that all injustices and inequality would be eliminated, that a "world order in which peace and justice and freedom" would reign supreme.

Jesse Jackson listened quietly, then rose to address the council. The blood stains were prominent on his sweater. He spoke with emotion. "A fitting memorial to King would be not to sit here looking sad and pious," Jackson began, "but to behave differently. This blood is on the chest and hands of those who would not have welcomed him here yesterday."

On Saturday morning, Jesse Jackson rose to speak to his usual crowd of Operation Breadbasket devotees in Chicago. But instead of the usual 400 people, there were 4,000 in attendance. Jackson spoke eloquently that morning, sending his message over the radio and being recorded on film. He spoke of carrying on the work of Dr. King, and of harmony between blacks and whites. His voice rose and fell with the intonations that King himself used, and his manner was very much like the slain leader's.

The time was ripe for this kind of approach. The blacks had been left without a leader to carry on King's programs against discrimination and poverty. The whites who had worked alongside the black men were afraid that the more militant voices within the movement would dominate. The Black Panthers and other groups, like Malcolm X's Black Muslims, had been advocating hatred of "whitey" and revolution for years. But Jesse Jackson managed to soothe the fears of most. His words were understandable, his manner radical yet acceptable. He was young, good-looking and nonviolent—incredibly charismatic. The world was looking for a leader, and many felt that Jackson was the natural choice to replace King.

Black leaders and spokesmen rose to speak on behalf of Jackson during those troubled days after King's death. Jackie Robinson said of Jackson that he was "another Martin Luther King, Jr.," that his goals were "those of all black America." The former mayor of Cleveland, Carl Stokes, said of Jackson: "He is the foremost civil rights spokesman in the country . . . a natural to assume leadership." Praise poured from the lips of black leaders throughout the country. The media, both television and print, picked up on Jesse Jackson as the heir apparent to King.

And it was with the media that Jackson rose quickly to the heights. It is interesting to examine why Jackson and the media worked so well together, especially during the weekend of April 4. With the death of King, the void had been created. The cameras and reporters did not know where to turn their attention. The black militants were frightening, especially to the white press. At a time when the black situation bordered on a mass explosion throughout the country, the "burn whitey burn" rhetoric of the militant blacks was deemed incendiary and dangerous. Jackson, however, was acceptable.

Martin Luther King, Jr., had been acceptable to the white press because of his religious views toward nonviolence. Everyone agreed that he was a good, decent man. King advocated change, but within the limits that the white man could understand and deal with. King made it possible to change without a race war, using his spiritual sense to elicit reform.

Jesse Jackson did not possess the spiritual sensibilities of a Martin Luther King. Few men did. What Jackson had to offer, however, was a perspective to which most of America could relate. Jackson, through Operation Breadbasket, the economic arm of the SCLC, had used economics to attack the problems confronting the blacks in Chicago. His entire power structure came not from threats of race wars, or condemnation in the afterlife, but instead from the very real and sensible threat of economic boycott. During his years in Chicago, Jackson had made his points very simply—give the black man jobs and a chance in the marketplace or else you will lose him as a customer. To much of white America Jackson was a businessman, not a theorist advocating impossible goals for the black man.

Jackson had always used the technique of economic force to push for his goals. He could sit down with white businessmen and speak their language, talk corporate profits and tax breaks. To the people living in Chicago's ghettos, he was a leader, a spiritual and charismatic man. But to the men who sat on the boards of America's large corporations, Jackson was a man who made a lot of sense. He was a man with whom they could speak and relate.

At the time of King's death, there were many people in the country who felt that King's power had decreased. Observers noted the rise in militancy, both among blacks and whites. Nonviolence was being seriously questioned as an effective means of effecting change. There were many who loved King, but looked upon him as a kindly old grandfather type who had long ago lost his potency. Malcolm X had called him "a glorious fool." And members of the Black Panthers had always questioned the effectiveness of nonviolence.

There was no doubt that King had raised the consciousness of a nation, that he had exposed the evils of prejudice and injustice which had reigned in the United States for over 300 years. To many of the young turks on their way up, King's role had been a glorious and effective one. But once the problems had been brought to the surface and exposed, then what? That is where the black movement began to splinter.

Malcolm X and his Black Muslim movement called for a race war, and for the development of a pure and intense hatred for the white man, the eternal oppressor of the black man. The Panthers called for a revolution, an armed revolt against the white oppressors. Splinter groups between the SCLC and the Muslims called for various forms of violence and armed confrontation.

Martin Luther King felt strongly that armed confrontation with the white man, aside from being spiritual suicide, would in fact result in racial suicide. King argued that the black man occupied only ten percent of the nation's populace, and would be annihilated in any kind of mass confrontation with the white power structure. Malcolm X argued that it was better to die a brave and fighting man than to die a thousand deaths as a coward. King argued that the only salvation for the black man was to remain spiritually pure, to not sink to the level of the white man and his violent, oppressive tactics.

The chasm within the black movement became wider

and wider, and at the time of King's death, was tremendous. The old guard from the SCLC advocated King's nonviolent program, while the militant blacks used King's death as a call to arms.

In this atmosphere emerged Jesse Jackson. His success in Chicago with Operation Breadbasket in creating jobs and making money flow into the black community gave Jackson a very real hook to hang his hat upon. His spiritual association with King gave him that abstract link that would allow him to pick up where King had left off. Jackson was the new wave as far as the movement was concerned. He was the missing link between the real economy and the spiritual and ethical demands of the Baptist preacher's mind. Jesse Jackson was a man of the seventies and eighties, and King had been a man of the fifties and sixties.

The white media felt the pulse of Jackson. He was very good on televiison. He was outspoken, photographed well, and spoke in eloquent terms about black pride and the need for the black man to become an economic success within the community. After hearing the threats of the militants, the media was ready for the ''American'' and very capitalistic voice of Jesse Jackson. Jackson was ready for them.

Ralph Abernathy, although annointed by King himself to take over the leadership of the SCLC, virtually disappeared from the media wires soon after King's death. The core of King's staff resented Jesse Jackson. They hated his media grabbing techniques, and referred to him as an opportunist.

Jesse Jackson was moving. He was a man who had groomed himself for leadership. He was a man who had carefully constructed an economic base in Chicago, one that provided him with almost total and complete access to the media. He was a man who did not wait for the inner council of the civil rights movement to await the emergence of a new leader, but instead seized a tragic moment in history and took hold of the reins when no one else was even reaching.

Is Jesse Jackson a cynical opportunist, playing power games with a people's struggle for freedom and justice? Or is he a natural extension of Martin Luther King, a man who is as suited to his time and role as was the great King himself?

We in this country have come to terms with leadership and the effect of power on mortal men. We have all heard the stories about John and Bobby Kennedy, and even the widespread rumors about King and his affairs with the ladies. We have grown up and come to understand that the kind of mind that seizes power is also the kind of mind that will appear opportunistic and Machiavellian. We have come to accept the fact a man must rule his own roost before he can be expected to effect change on a broader scale. Is Jesse Jackson the kind of leader who possesses the guile and the shrewdness necessary to be effective? Or, as many claimed during the weeks after King's death, is he dangerous because he is able to justify the end with the means?

That first week in April of 1968 saw a shift in power within the black civil rights movement that is still sending waves of change throughout the country. Ralph Abernathy slid into a virtual oblivion while Jesse Jackson emerged as the newest Messiah. Today, Jackson is the spokesman for black America. Many call him the most powerful black man in the world. He is Jesse Jackson, and as he likes to say at his rallies, he is "somebody." But just who is this man who has captured the imagination, and become power broker, of millions of people throughout the world?

Chapter 2

Beginnings

On the quiet streets of Greenville, South Carolina, in 1941 there walked a black man who dared everyone in the small Southern town to call him "mister." Noah Louis Robinson was a large man, handsome and incredibly popular with the ladies, but he was also a proud man, and the citizens of Greenville respected him. Both black and white alike called him Mister Robinson.

Mr. Robinson was married to a woman who had three children by a previous marriage. He wanted a boy of his own—his wife was unable to give it to him—so Noah Robinson turned to a pretty young woman who lived next door by the name of Helen Burns. Helen conceived, and on October 8, 1941, she gave birth to a healthy baby boy. The boy was named Jesse Louis Burns.

The birth was a happy one for both Heln Burnes and Noah Robinson. But the trauma for Helen was just beginning. Still a student in high school at the time of Jesse's birth, Helen became the target of small town gossip and hate. Many felt she should have aborted her child rather than face the stigma of having a child out of wedlock. The town became so opposed to Helen's open stand that they kicked her out of the Baptist Church which she had attended throughout her life.

Noah Robinson supported Helen and his son, and he openly took "credit" for Jesse, but he did not marry the young girl. Instead, he boasted of his son.

Today, Jesse Jackson speaks about the origins of his birth with great candor. On his Saturday morning broadcasts in Chicago, he will often refer to the man who lived next door, could not have a "man-child" of his own, and consequently went next door looking for it. There are those who condemn Jackson's candor on this matter, saying that a "bastard" should never boast of his origins. They say that Jackson should drop the subject because it results in a sense of moral outrage in many of Greenville's citizens, even to this day.

Jesse Jackson's honesty over his birth is quite possibly motivated by a much more practical goal than to outrage the townspeople who ridiculed him throughout his childhood. The illegitimate birthrate among blacks in America is disproportionately high when compared to that of whites. Psychological analysis of the black man has conjured up a vision of men working and struggling against great odds;

men whose pride in their ability to support their children has been stripped away by the "racist" society in which they live. It is a common phenomenon within the black community for women to bear children without having the father around. Also, because of the extremely high unemployment rate among blacks, it is not uncommon for the father to "disappear" into the streets in order to allow the mother to collect monetary benefits from the state and federal welfare programs. Decisions like this are made every day, the kind that come from a father thinking that it is better to abandon his family to the welfare rolls than to allow his children to starve to death on his meager salary.

Consequently, there are a large number of black children who, like Jesse Jackson, remain fatherless throughout their lives. Jackson did not know who his father was until after most of his childhood had passed and the abuse of the town had been heaped upon him. His candor on this matter is probably quite effective in providing other children who suffer the same fate with a sense of identity and a loss of alienation.

Jesse Jackson knows all about identity and alienation. In 1943, his mother finally married. The man's name was Charles Henry Jackson. An easy-going man, Charles Jackson supported his new family in a decent and modest style. For Jesse's mother, Helen, the marriage literally stopped the town's gossiping and ridicule. Now, she was ensconsed within an acceptable and legal marriage, and people stopped talking about her in hushed whispers.

For little Jesse, the route of discovery was just beginning. Jesse had a younger stepbrother, Noah Junior, who lived next door with his real father, Noah Robinson. Noah did not know that he had a brother in Jesse, and only through local gossip did he find out. He was seven years old at the time, only ten months younger than Jesse. His discovery would eventually lead to Jesse's discovery.

For most of his early life, Jesse thought of Charles Jackson as his real father. The gossip, plus Noah's knowledge, finally brought home the fact that Jesse had been born out of wedlock. According to those who were with him at the time, the youngster was affected deeply by the knowledge. As he moved into his first decade of life, Jesse began to sense what he was missing with his real family. Although he loved his mother and stepfather, he would oftentimes stand for hours outside the home of the man who had fathered him. As if being left out, Jesse would watch the Robinson family as they went through their daily routines. Deep within his active mind, Jesse must have known that he was being excluded—that somehow, he had been left out, that his family life was not to be a normal one.

It is probably for the reasons of his origin that Jesse Jackson developed into the powerful individual that he is today. Racism in Greenville, South Carolina, during those years was not as rampant or oppressive as to drive a young man into direct aciton against its injustices. The town was born around a textile mill and had a population of over 60,000 people. The whites owned the factory, and the blacks worked inside and at various other trades. Greenville was segregated, but there was little of the racial tension that existed in other parts of the South. The blacks lived in modest homes on tree-lined streets, and some were fairly well off.

Jackson's natural father, Noah Robinson, had come from a line of Baptist preachers, the church being the birthplace of the black middle class at that time. Noah Robinson himself was a respected man, even among the whites. He was treated fairly, and he was well-liked. Even with the town tongues shaming him over the birth of Jesse, he still retained the respect of the white businessmen with whom he worked.

Although racism existed on a peaceful level in Greenville, the times were changing. The town would accommodate the blacks as long as they remained subservient and peaceful. Greenville did not integrate until the sixties, but even then, it was done in a peaceful manner.

Living and growing up in this environment began to form within Jesse Jackson a sense of identity as a black man. Jesse suffered through a kind of dual allegiance to his stepfather and his real father, and it seems that he chose to align himself with the black man in total, instead of just one individual. A quick and active child, with a bent towards athletics, Jackson began to see himself as a black, as somebody who would not tolerate bad service or ridicule from his peers and elders.

There are a lot of stories which come out of Jesse Jackson's childhood that attest to his audacious nature: times when he walked into stores demanding quick service, other instances when he would stare down opponents and cut them to the quick with a word. Jesse Jackson was, indeed, the kind of child who moved fast and hard through his early years.

Home life for Jackson began to sow the seeds which

would later result in his drive and ambition, not to mention his ability and need to work eighteen hours a day. Jesse's grandmother, a Southern woman with respect for the Bible and decency, taught Jesse and his younger brother, Charles, the meaning and spiritual necessity of working. Jesse loved his grandmother, and took her advice. At the age of six, he was already employed. At the age of eight, Jackson had begun working as a concessionaire at the local football stadium, the first black to ever work there in that capacity. By the time Jesse was nine, he was elected to the National Sunday School Convention in Charlotte. There, little Jesse would stand before the other members and make his report. It was his first public speaking engagement, and he was extremely successful at it.

As Jackson matured into puberty, many of his friends noted his attitude toward whites. They would recount Jesse speaking of the white man in humorous, derogatory terms. Jackson himself remembers listening to the fights of Joe Louis, praying silently that the great Black Hope would win, afraid to speak out publicly for his hero. Jackson also remembers living in a segregated world, where black children would deny their own thirst because of the "white only" signs over drinking fountains. Jackson seemed to have a grip on what was happening around him, one that saw through the hypocrisy and injustice of segregation. His personality at the time was one which would naturally rebel and joke about his position.

Although during those years Jackson's political thoughts were not developed, he began to build within himself a sense of participation and ambition that would never leave.

In high school, Jackson, an acclaimed athlete, began to run for whatever school office was open. In the ninth grade, his classmates elected him to the office of student body president. Jackson was also the star quarterback at his high school, rated by his coach as the finest quarterback he'd ever coached.

Jesse Jackson, the high school student, was a climber. He dressed immaculately, and held himself in high esteem. He was a battler, a doer and a success. His teachers enjoyed him, although they found him to be mischievous and oftentimes unruly. He was popular with his classmates, although they oftentimes found his intense drive to succeed somewhat overbearing. Jackson was the kind of high school student whom many hated, just because he was so openly ambitious and so inclined to throw himself into whatever battle loomed on the horizon. He was a good speaker, and eloquent. Jackson would study the dictionary just to improve his vocabulary and learn to speak better. His words were used not so much for advancement of the black man as they were used to woo the females and put down his opponents.

There were a lot of students who might have called Jackson a "kiss ass" during his years in high school. But Jackson's activities on the streets prevented that. He was a good crap shooter, a veritable rabble rouser and genuinely a leader of men, even if at that time most were boys. Jackson's sense of the good time was developed even then, a quality which carries over today.

Jesse Jackson's years in high school read like an all-American dream. Handsome, athletic, and academically successful, Jackson was one of those who should have won the award for most likely to succeed upon graduation. Everyone has had experience with a student like Jackson, the student who seems to have everything. Many students will remember hearing about those popular ''big men on campus'' years later, how they ended up with a mortgage, three children and a job as a truck driver. Not Jesse Jackson. Whatever was driving Jesse during his years in high school would not let go after graduation. The ambition and talent which quickly showed itself within him would remain.

There is speculation as to why Jesse Jackson was the kind of youth he was. The most logical stems from the situation which existed at his birth. Jesse was a child who did not have the security of a natural family, a child who grew up looking to himself for his sense of identity and accomplishment. Stories emerging from his childhood tell of the intense competition which existed between Jesse and his brother Noah, how the two were continually at each others' throats, trying desperately to outdo the other. Psychologically, it could be said that Jesse was vying for the love and attention of his natural father, trying to steal that which belonged to Noah. But it is more complex than that.

Jesse Jackson was a bright, talented child let loose in a world with two strikes against him. First, being the ''illegitimate'' son of Noah Robinson; and secondly, being black in the South. Being as aware as he was, Jesse reacted against these two strikes not by succumbing but by trying to beat the system. His attitudes were always aggressive, his style was always play to win. Jackson could have easily stumbled in another direction, into the nightmare world of self-pity and drugs. He could have given up on himself and his life and wandered aimlessly down a road laden with rejection and despair.

The ego which so many people complain about, however, took Jesse Jackson down a road which eventually would result in him becoming the most powerful leader of blacks in the country. The ego which demanded that people take notice; the ego which prompted him to run for every student body office; the ego which pushed him to excel at athletics—it is the same ego which emerges every Saturday morning in Chicago when Jackson stands before the microphones and praises his own, as well as others' individuality with the phrase, "I am Somebody!"

Jesse Jackson has developed an ego that works, an ego that moves forward. He has shown many blacks how to integrate their selfish needs for creature comforts and pleasures into a workable partnership with larger goals. He has demonstrated an old theory of society that the individual, through personal selfishness, is the only solution to the ills of a nation.

Where did Jesse Jackson combine that ego which led him to success in high school with the movement itself? How did he manage to find the junction between his own goals and desires and those of an entire nation of oppressed black men and women?

The awareness of racism came early, during his childhood when Jackson noted the effects of segregation. His attitude towards whites, as mentioned previously, was one of scorn. He saw injustice, but most likely, in his young mind he did not see the reasons. He only knew it existed, and for a boy of Jackson's ego, it was most likely a personal affront rather than a national disease.

The personal affront hit Jesse Jackson on a financial level upon graduation from Sterling High in Greenville in 1959. A star athlete, Jackson was offered a contract to play baseball for the New York Giants. The American League's Chicago White Sox countered and outbid the Giants, offering Jackson $6,000 to play for them. At the time, it seemed like a good offer. When Jackson heard that Dickie Dietz, a white ballplayer, had received an offer of $90,000 from the same Chicago club, he grew irate. For the first time in his life, Jackson realized that the white man draws more money on the marketplace than the black man. It was an obvious injustice, and one that would stay with Jackson throughout his life.

So, instead of playing major league ball, Jesse Jackson decided to reject the offers and accept an athletic scholarship to the University of Illinois. Having come from his high school as an exceptional quarterback, Jackson was determined to play in the Big Ten in the same position. What had been racism in the South now reared its ugly head in the North. Another instance of a cruel awakening, Jackson was told that the Big Ten did not accept blacks as quarterbacks. The team leader would be a white player, the running backs would be black. Once again, Jackson saw that injustice existed everywhere. Even on the campus, he was subjected to the division between the white students and the blacks. Being the kind of man Jackson was, used to having his way and loving the glow of popularity, he began rejecting the status quo. One year at the University of Illinois and Jesse Jackson transferred to the black Agriculture and Technical College of North

Carolina at Greensboro.

Back home in the South, Jesse Jackson reclaimed his own sense of identity and his ego. He became a star quarterback on the football team and won many honors as President of the Student Body. He was popular again, being the center of attention. The girls loved him, and Jackson returned the compliment. Jesse Jackson, living among his black brothers and sisters, was home again.

Home in Greensboro provided Jesse Jackson with a forum that would eventually project him into the national limelight as a hero of the Civil Rights Movement. Before his arrival in the college town, four protesters had walked into a Woolworth's luncheon counter. The year was 1960. The four students were black. Segregation was the accepted norm, and the four students were asked to leave the counter. Instead of capitulating to what had been a hundred years of societal law, the four students retained their seats, opened their textbooks and began to read. The sit-in was born.

In 1963, Jesse Jackson arrived on the campus in Greensboro. Quickly, he established himself as a leader. Star quarterback, ladies' man and all-around romantic figure. Instead of resting on his laurels, however, Jackson involved himself in the Civil Rights Movement. At the time, the Congress of Racial Equality (CORE) was handling and organizing the sit-ins and demonstrations in Greensboro. Jackson, in his usual audacious way, went to the leadership and complained that they were not doing the job. Jackson was dared to be more effective.

The success which Jackson achieved during those early years of the movement would provide a clue to his future.

Jackson organized Greensboro over the next ten months, leading a continuous chain of sit-ins and demonstrations. He was arrested for inciting a riot in the downtown area and sent to jail. Jackson's flair for the dramatic had already emerged during this period. He spoke of himself in terms of the martyr, being punished for his beliefs. His charisma was evident; students would follow him. He was a success in his first venture into the movement, and people throughout the black chain of power began to take notice.

Because of Jackson's success in Greensboro, he was elected President of the North Carolina Intercollegiate Council on Human Rights. In his senior year, Jesse Jackson penetrated the power councils of the movement when he was named field director for the Southeastern sections. It was at this time that Jesse Jackson met James Farmer, Floyd McKissick and other blacks who were instrumental in the movement. Jackson began inching closer and closer to the top man himself, the Reverend Martin Luther King, Jr.

College had started a path for Jackson that would eventually take him to the leadership of the entire movement. He had opted for a black school instead of a white Northern university, and he had begun to assume leadership. During that period of time, in 1962, Jackson married, another step that was to solidify his commitment. The lady was a beautiful girl named Jacqueline Lavinia Davis, a radical on campus who related to Jesse on a political level, only to have the romance blossom at a later time. His marriage, and his commitment to the movement set the stage for Jackson, gave him a path and direction, which he would travel for nearly two decades, and who knows how much longer than that.

Jesse Jackson had come a long way since his high school days. He had ventured into the white man's world, had been presented with the opportunity to play major league baseball and had been presented with an opportunity to star as a running back at the University of Illinois. Jackson turned the white man down. He had opted for a black college, and had immersed himself with the Civil Rights Movement. His strong instinct, not to mention his ego, had spoken to him, and Jesse Jackson had listened. By the time he graduated from A&T, Jesse Jackson would be labeled a "comer" within the movement, a young turk capable of drawing crowds, organizing demonstrations and being an effective leader of men.

During this time, as Jackson began rising through the movement itself, he began to understand his calling, a calling to which his natural grandfather had responded; and a calling to which Martin Luther King had responded. Years of struggle lay ahead, the movement awaited him, and Jesse Jackson began to seriously consider becoming a preacher. It was a decision that would serve to bring together the talents and aspirations of this ambitious, driving man who would quickly rise to the heights of power within the movement.

Following the death of Dr. Martin Luther King, Jesse Jackson quickly took charge of the Civil Rights Movement, much to the chagrin of other black leaders.

44

Chapter 3

The Movement

By 1963, Jesse Jackson had decided to become a preacher. Although he had wavered between politics and the ministry, seriously considering going to Duke and studying law, the calling had come. As a matter of fact, it had been in his mind since the age of fourteen.

Jackson was a little miffed that the idea did not pop with a fanfare and bugle call. Instead, it had been a notion that had been developing within him for years, quietly at first, then with greater and greater emphasis as he came to adore and eventually emulate his father figure hero, Martin Luther King.

In 1964, Jackson enrolled in the Chicago Theology

Seminary to study for the ministry, but retreating into the seclusion of the scholarly life was not Jesse's style. While in Chicago, he became more and more active within the movement, joining the Southern Christian Leadership Conference as one of King's young and energetic lieutenants.

During the early sixties, Martin Luther King's SCLC had made great advances in the South. The march on Birmingham, with its legendary stand against Bull Connors, had created for King and his movement widespread fame. With the newsreel footage depicting the heavy-set southern Sheriff Connors, training his fire hoses and dogs on negro demonstrators, the Birmingham marches probably did more to raise the white man's consciousness towards civil rights than any incident which had come before.

King and his staff, then including Ralph Abernathy and Andy Young, were moving forcefully and with good results through the South. Integration was occurring in one southern bastion of racism after another. With each success in the South, King was gaining power and fame.

During 1965, King led his forces into Selma and called upon his people throughout America to gather together as many foot soldiers as possible for the march to Montgomery. At the time, Jesse Jackson was in Chicago, supporting King, talking on his behalf, and moving more and more into an active role within the SCLC. Upon hearing King's call for manpower, Jackson miraculously organized over one half of the student body of the theology school and brought them to Selma.

King and his aides were duly impressed. Ralph

Abernathy remembered Jackson as an intense, energetic worker, a dedicated disciple who was willing to do anything to get involved. It was, ironically enough, Abernathy who recommended to King that Jesse Jackson be given greater responsibility. Andy Young remembers Jackson from that march, remembers how Jackson complimented him on an essay he had written. The young man from Chicago was impressing everyone.

King was also impressed, even when Jackson stepped onto the steps of a city building to join with King and Abernathy to give a speech. No one had invited Jesse Jackson to speak that day. As a matter of fact, only the staff members of the SCLC had been invited to talk to the enthusiastic crowds, but Jesse Jackson took it upon himself to address the people. He pulled it off. Reaction to his speech was almost as positive as it had been to King's. Reporters from across the country made a note of the young man, and his ability to churn the emotions of a crowd.

The final coup for Jackson during the Selma march was to be able to speak directly with King. The Doctor was impressed with Jesse, and liked his energy and dedication. King was alone. Even with his ability to placate and compliment, Jesse Jackson was far from being a favorite among King's staffers. Most felt, even then, that he was too ambitious, too much of a gadfly. They had all been on the marches, been beaten and thrown into jail. They had suffered through the dogs, the fire hoses and the abuse of the racist South. Jackson had not. Yet, here he was, in conference with King, making speeches with the top leaders of the SCLC and getting his name in all the papers.

Resentment began to grow against Jesse Jackson.

Whatever the staffers felt, Jesse Jackson was walking his own road. Whether by coincidence or strategy, Jackson had ended up in Chicago. While King and his loyal troops concentrated all of their efforts in the deep South, Jesse Jackson had been building a foundation in the North. This simple fact would prove to be Jackson's catapult to fame.

As racism became a well-known fact in America during the late fifties and early sixties, the majority of Americans looked to the South for its roots. Most whites would conjure up images of Bull Connors, poor blacks in Mississippi and the white hoods of the Klan as the earmarks of racism. The South, because of its revolt against the Union and its economy based on the enslavement of the black man, was considered the most racist part of the country. The South had "colored only" drinking fountains and restrooms, and the southern restaurants and coffee shops would not serve "coloreds." Racism in the South had been easy to spot, and had provided an easy target for the northern liberals.

The feeling in the North, as it had been since the days of the Civil War, was one of superiority. Northerners automatically assumed that they were liberal humanitarians while the Southerners were bigoted racists. Nothing could have been further from the truth.

Racism in the North did not reveal itself in segregated drinking fountains or blacks crammed into the back of buses. There were no lonely country roads were lynch mobs in white hoods carried a black man to a hanging tree. The racism in the North revealed itself instead by the suffocating, deadly slums were black people "lived," the ghettos.

The Northern ghettos had emerged after the Emancipation Proclamation when blacks became "free" to leave the South and the plantation and head north to the industrial capitals of America. They went north until like all immigrants seeking entry into a society, they began to huddle together in the rundown, cheap areas of the cities. In New York, they massed together in Harlem. In Chicago, they moved to the Southside and Westside. In the far West, they congregated on the bleak southern edge of Los Angeles; and in San Francisco, they moved across the bay to the industrial area known as Oakland.

As the twentieth century moved forward, the blacks living in the ghettos began to suffer. The industries around them boomed; the men had work, but there were no laws regulating pay. The blacks made less money for the same jobs than the white man. Schools began to deteriorate. Money from municipal bonds went to the white schools, not to the inner city centers of education. The neighborhoods grew. Landlords pulled as much rent out of the poor blacks in the cities as they could manage. As the midpoint in the century arrived, the blacks were crowded, poor and with growing desperation, locked into the neighborhoods that were rotting with hopelessness and frustration.

The Northern cities watched the growing Civil Rights Movement in the South with an almost peculiar air of detachment, as though Birmingham and Selma were strange little Third World countries, with odd little people fighting themselves. The northern media loved to play liberal with the movement in the South, and films depicting Bull Connor characterizations of racist southern mentality were increasingly popular. The North had its negroes, but the North was still the land of freedom and opportunity. At least that's how the Northerners loved to see themselves.

The North, according to the northern politicians, was not in the least racist. Negroes were allowed to sit with whites at ball games; were not forbidden to drink from water fountains; were allowed to travel with whites; and were even courted in Harlem and Chicago for their music and soul. The North was not racist because the North did not have the Ku Klux Klan.

In the summer of 1965, something happened in the North which northerners could not understand. During a devastatingly hot summer, blacks in Watts took to the streets and began burning down their own businesses, throwing rocks at policemen, and indulging in an orgy of violence and bloodshed. Suddenly, the country was shocked into an awakening. It became painfully obvious to many that the problems and frustration which had pained the blacks in the South were just as real, and quite possibly even more lethal, in the North.

Studies were compiled in an attempt to analyze just why the riots had broken out. Some attributed the eruption to a hot summer. More insightful thinkers began to see where the problems had begun. the hope for freedom and a reasonable life had evaded the blacks in the North. They had been forced into the ghettos, living in an urban hell, blocked on all sides by concrete and despair. Children were starving in these ghettos, and black men were seething with frustration. Drugs were abundant everywhere, and white dealers were celebrating the hopelessness of the black ghetto dweller in their villas in the South of France. The masses which had migrated to the North were now paying their dues. They were being exploited, confined into horrendous housing, and left to die in the nightmare world of the inner cities.

There were no easy solutions to the massive problem. The South, after years of rebuilding and wooing the northern industries, was beginning very quickly to regain a financial base. Jobs were abundant, and once the traditional racist ideologies had been broken down, many blacks found themselves gainfully employed. Also, the South did not possess the hellish ghettos of the North—the Harlems, the Westsides and the Wattses. The South was generally a prettier place to live, a country atmosphere. One need only compare the two industrial giants, Birmingham and Detroit, to see the difference.

The problems in the North, then, were seemingly far more complex than those in the South. Racism existed on a much more subtle scale than it did in the South. Suburbs refused housing to blacks, not on legal edicts, but on economic manipulation based on the fear that a black family would mean lower property values to a neighborhood. Unemployment in the cities was higher, and so what if blacks suffered the most? The white man also suffered. Then there was the problem with the police. The Northern cities were concrete jungles, their streets were hidden and unexplored rivers of asphalt where men preyed upon one another far from the public eye. In the deepest, darkest corners of Harlem or Chicago's Westside, a man may be bludgeoned to death and not be found for weeks. The white press, comprised of men afraid of the dangers of the ghetto, rarely ventured into the black communities to cover a story. The death of a black man in Harlem would bring no coverage while the murder of a white man in Scarsdale would make headlines.

The ghettos have often been called concentration camps without barbed wire. A man and his family, once ensconced, find escape almost impossible. In the ghetto, the power structure for the people comes from the street, while the municipal laws which govern food, rent and jobs come from city hall. The ghetto dweller must fight both his counterpart in the jungle and the man in the mayor's seat simultaneously. The power for change is not easily created. Survival is often the only goal of the ghetto dweller. He neither thinks in terms of politics, nor will act if given the opportunity during an election. In Watts and Harlem, and later in Detroit and Chicago, the black man in the ghetto was more prone to violence than to the voting booth.

Martin Luther King had been tremendously effective in the South, but the ghettos remained a mystery to him. They were huge, nightmarish sprawls of waste and concrete, populated by more blacks than lived in the South.

To Jesse Jackson, the ghettos of Chicago were becoming home. He was getting to know the city in which he lived, learning who controlled what and beginning to understand what it was that made Richard Daley the most powerful mayor in the history of the nation.

It was this understanding, and this background that would prepare Jesse Jackson to make giant forward leaps in the movement. This background would eventually lead Jackson to become the spokesman for the nation's black population.

The first test of Jesse Jackson's effectiveness in the North would come with the arrival of Martin Luther King in Chicago. For years, King had demonstrated his effectiveness in the South, and now, it was time to expand his operation. King knew that he needed a national base of departure, and he knew that Chicago was the city to provide him with it. King had long ago christened Chicago the capital of northern segregation. Now it was time to deal with the North. The year was 1966.

The people of Chicago were shocked at King's plans to come to their city to protest the state of human rights. Richard Daley, the kingpin and mayor, had declared Chicago to be a city which did not have any segregation. "We recognize every man, regardless of race, national origin, or creed," Daley had said. "And they are entitled to their rights as provided in the United States Constitution and the Constitution of Illinois." Daley had spoken, and so had congressmen, and city councilmen. Even a black congressman, William Dawson, had warned King to stay out of Chicago. It seemed that everyone in Chicago knew exactly what their situation was, and that King was making waves only for the sake of creating turbulence.

The Daley machine, however, not the people, was speaking. Richard Daley had not come to be regarded as the most powerful mayor in America for nothing. Over the years in which he had served the windy city as its mayor, Daley had built a political machine unequaled anywhere. Almost every politician and civic leader was in Daley's pocket. His system of buying votes and controlling wards on the local levels by actually paying voters off at the polls with chickens, wine and cigars had gained him a sturdy lock on Chicago politics. With the legacy of Al Capone, there were very few who would dare question the stocky little mayor.

Martin Luther King was ready, so he believed, for the political strength of Mayor Daley. King knew that at a convention of the NAACP Daley had claimed that there were no ghettos in Chicago. As ridiculous as this statement seemed at the time, Daley uttered it with a straight face. No one called him on it. It seemed that in Chicago if Daley told the people that he was Jesus Christ, enough would cater to his statement to publicly release it as fact.

So, with Daley denying the existence of ghettos and controlling the Cook County machine, King was waiting anxiously to make his move. He found his chance with the ongoing controversy over Chicago's superintendent of education, Benjamin Willis. Willis had gained notoriety for refusing to integrate Chicago's schools. He had even gone so far as to lease trailers for the black children to study in rather than allow them into the same classrooms with whites. Willis was a true villain, a nasty and cartoonish counterpart of the Bull Connors of the South. He was perfect for King.

A man named Al Raby, at the time head of the Coordinating Council of Community Organizations (CCCO), had been doing battle with Willis. Raby had linked together a somewhat powerful group of demonstrators to protest the actions of Willis. His thousands of marchers soon dwindled down to a precious few. Daley's tactics in combating Raby had been simple—to ignore him most of the time, and when he did pay attention, to treat him as though were mentally deranged. Daley used the tactic efectively, and Raby began losing support. He put in a phone call to Martin Luther King and begged the national leader to come to Chicago and help him out.

King realized than an opportunity was presenting itself to him in Chicago. He desperately wanted, at the time, to nationalize his SCLC and bring it to the attention of the country, and, especially, the Northern cities. King announced his plans to come to Chiago to do battle with the evil Willis.

Mayor Daley heard of King's plans to invade his city and promptly went into action. He stole the thunder from King's arrival, and Raby's years of protest, by relieving Willis of his post. Daley knew that the news media, following on King's heels, would love nothing better than footage and snapshots of black children huddled together in Willis' trailers. Daley knew that they would love nothing better than to listen to Willis' promise to never integrate Chicago's public schools. Daley knew that Willis would have to go, so off went the evil destroyer of children's education.

For many in the movement, the firing of Willis was looked upon as a victory. Those who understood Daley knew that the Mayor was playing tactical games, and had virtually destroyed King's chances of marching into his city with a direct, visually accessible purpose. If King was coming to Chicago, Daley must have thought, he'll have to come and speak about abstract things like spiritual dignity and human rights.

King knew he had been stymied. He began searching for an issue, one that would hit directly at the gut of the

Northern city. In council with his staff and advisors, the King men decided on open housing, one of the most sensitive issues in any major urban area. King called his new crusade "The Campaign To End Slums."

Almost immediately following the announcement of the new campaign, Mayor Daley addressed the nation via the media and explained with zeal that Chicago would do everything within its power to eradicate slums, and that by 1967, there would be no more slums within the city of Chicago.

King was at an impasse with the Mayor. Also, he had never come up against a trickster like king Richard before. Daley had once denied the existence of slums, and then had spoken about eradicating them. It was as though Daley would say whatever would work to stifle the movement and keep the peace. King could not understand what this man was up to. He could not understand why people fell for the obvious lies.

Jesse Jackson, then working with CCCO and the SCLC while attending theology school, would not be able to give King a rational explanation either. All Jesse Jackson knew at the time was what he saw and heard with his own eyes.

Throughout King's success lay a basic pattern in which demonstrations and effective massing of protesters existed. This pattern always began with the local church, mostly the Baptist preachers who loved and respected King. They would receive word from King's advance men that the Reverend was coming to town to march for this, or to demonstrate for that. The preachers would pass the word to their congregations, and when King arrived, he would have his troops in line and ready to march.

In Chicago, the problem of getting the local ministers together to support King was much more complex. Most of the black men of God had long ago come to grip with the all-powerful Daley machine, and had learned to live with its evil. Daley's political genius rested in his ability to persuade, one way or the other, leaders of small groups of people to join his camp. Daley needed the vote of the people, but more than that, he needed the preachers, the local businessmen, the doctors and lawyers—all those who, in one way or the other affected the thinking of their communities. Daley's sucess in the black Westside and Southside of Chicago came as a direct reult of his having most of the local preachers living comfortably with his machine. Promises of new, modern churches, the donation of city facilities for one fund raiser or another that would elevate the minister in the eye of his church—all those gratuities were thrust upon the local man who could produce the votes.

So, when King announced his upcoming crusade into Chicago, he received very little support from the local black clergy. Daley had warned them, and they knew that by stepping out of the Daley camp into the King camp, they would be sacrificing years of building a rapport with the Daley machine.

There were other, more abstract reasons why King did not receive the support of Chicago's ministers. Jesse Jackson had debated going into the ministry for this very reason—that many black clergymen were devoted to the idea of heaven after death instead of heaven on earth. Jackson hated this attitude, feeling that it was little more than a compromise to the realities of injustice. Also, there was a lot of resentment towards King and his men on the part of the ministers. Many of these men felt that they had learned to live as best they could with a difficult situation, and that King and his men were gaining all the headlines and notoriety by making their lives more difficult and upsetting the delicate balance which they had achieved.

Jesse Jackson's reaction to all of this was simple: he would go to these men, speak with them directly and make them feel their manliness again. That is the essential secret of Jesse Jackson, the one quality which has always separated him from an Abernathy. Jackson has the ability to conjure the decency and honor within a man that may have long been buried deep inside. He is able to make people stand up and declare themselves to be ''somebody'' without forcing them to pick up a rifle. During the weeks prior to King's arrival in Chicago, Jackson worked day and night talking with the local ministers, pleading and begging, cajoling and arguing, and finally bringing a great many of them to their feet. They were standing and waiting when, in July of 1966, Jesse Jackson greeted Martin Luther King and his aides at O'Hare Airport in a limousine.

King's move into Chicago was highly successful at first, due mainly to Jackson's ability to organize local support. A rally held at Soldier Field on July 11, drew nearly 60,000 people. Later a successful march was conducted into the Loop, where King nailed up a petition on the door of the mayor's office which called for forty demands on open and fair housing.

The demands called for open housing, non-discriminatory mortgages, a citizens group to investigate police brutality, and minority hiring in the craft unions.

Daley, once again on the hot seat, jumped off. He explained to King that there was already a program in Chicago for cleaning up the ghettos. King ignored the mayor and waited.

Five days after the rally, some children on Chicago's Southside inadvertently started a riot in an attempt to get cool in the sweltering heat. The kids turned on some fire hydrants. The police moved against them, and the kids reacted. The National Guard was called out, and King was blamed for the riot. Daley inferred that the leader had come to Chicago to get children to riot.

The heat dropped, and Daley and King sat in Chicago staring at one another. King was afraid of another riot because of the heat, and asked the mayor to provide some kind of relief to the black children during the hot summer months. Daley understood. He felt if he could keep King and his people off his back by turning the fire hydrants on, then he would certainly go that far.

King was stalemated once again by Daley. He took his wife and family and moved into a Southside apartment to show the world the conditions under which Chicago blacks had to live. Daley immediately sent a crew in to repair the apartment and give it a new paint job.

King was being pushed against a wall by Daley, and he decided to act. He announced his decision to take the forces which had amassed behind him and march into Chicago's blue-collar, white neighborhoods. Daley was riled. He knew what the reaction of these people would be, and he knew that he, the mayor, would be thrown into the middle. The blacks would riot again if he stopped King, and the whites would be furious at him for allowing the "niggers" into their neighborhoods.

In August of 1966, King marched into Chicago's Gage Park on the city's south side. What greeted the black demonstrators was what many called the ugliest demonstration of hatred toward blacks they had ever seen. Housewives, children and workers hung out of windows and placed themselves on rooftops, yelling and screaming obscenities at the marchers.

The march was a horror, but it prompted mayor Daley to call King back to the negotiation table. Daley then offered a package deal, one that was designed to make the mayor appear to be a savior of the black man while at the same time offering the movement literally nothing in return. King refused to sign the agreement, and the meeting, which included Jesse Jackson, broke up with King promising to take his marchers deeper and deeper into the white neighborhoods.

Marquette Park was King's next target. This time, the local citizenry reacted by hurtling bricks at the marchers. Jesse Jackson was hit by one of the bricks, and therefore duly initiated into Chicago politics.

The next march took place in Cragin, another blue-collar neighborhood. This time, the reaction of the crowd became a distressing sign of things to come for the mayor. The crowds had been separated into blacks and whites, the marchers moving between them. At one point in the march, the whites broke through the police lines in an attempt to reach the blacks on the other side of the street. The Chicago police blocked their way, and on the news that night there were vivid pictures of Chicago's finest beating white citizens with nightsticks.

Daley was heartsick. The last thing in the world he wanted was to have his white voting bloc think that he was sicking his own police on them. On the blacks, well, that was something else. But on whites? It wouldn't be until the Chicago Democratic Convention some two years in the future that people would believe it when they saw Chicago cops maiming white youngsters. For the moment, however, Daley had to preserve his image.

King and his people, because of the riot on the Cragin march, now had the momentum. Daley was quickly being forced into the middle, the one position from which he could not act. Daley would do anything to stay out of the crunch.

What really forced the issue was the decision to march on Cicero, an all-white community that had once violently expelled a negro couple who were attempting to buy a home there. And what really forced the Cicero issue was Jesse Jackson.

Plans had been formulating to march on Cicero for some time, but King's staff was waiting for exactly the right moment. According to sources, Jesse Jackson jumped the gun and enthusiastically proclaimed to the press that King would march on Cicero. The reaction was one of startled disbelief from both Daley's office and from the office of King. King's staffers were not that stricken; they had long been complaining about Jackson's ability and seemingly endless ambition to steal headlines.

King was forced into a position. He either had to publicly embarrass Jackson, or support the intention of marching in that all-white community. King decided on the latter, explaining to the press that Cicero was, indeed, their next goal.

Although many on the staff felt that Jackson had blundered terribly, the statement did bring the Chicago effort to a critical stage much quicker than if nothing had been said. Mayor Daley, knowing that he was being pushed against the wall, and knowing how well Cicero loved the idea of "niggers" marching through its streets, issued an injunction limiting the marchers to 500, while implementing a curfew.

King ignored Daley's move and told him that he would produce the greatest number of marchers Chicago had ever seen. He wasn't about to be stopped by an eleventh hour injunction.

Daley took a deep breath and invited King, Jackson and the rest of the staff back to the negotiation tables. As the powerbrokers of the SCLC met with the kingpin of Chicago, the world waited. The result of the conference was the acceptance of King's open housing pact by Mayor Daley.

It looked like a total victory for King, Jackson and the rest. King called the agreement a "total eradication of housing discrimination." Daley chimed in with: "This is a great day in the history of our city."

Throughout the movement, the general consensus was that King had Mayor Daley on the run. Elections were less than a year away, and Daley had been forced into what at the time was considered a major concession. King was urged by his staff and other leaders to go for the jugular, to mount a drive that would oust Daley from his position of power and forever reshape the politics of Chicago.

A series of realizations after the signing of the open housing pact between King and Daley, however, began a backslide for the movement in the windy city from which King and his forces would never quite recover. After the elation over the agreement had died and men began seriously questioning it, they discovered that what they had signed was literally nothing more than a bureaucratic plan for avoiding the issues. There were no real, hard programs within the agreement, merely a closet full of committees and loopholes. One aide said that what they had wanted was definite statements that apartments in the slums would be monitored, and repairs made once a year; that mortgage companies would come under federal control insofar as their licenses went in order to avoid any discrimination; that a guarantee of equal employment would be enforced throughout the city, using federal loans and other powers of outside money as leverage. What the movement got, however, was words and a whole lot of them. One worker within the movement complained at the time that he was barely able to understand the agreement, much less comment on whether or not it would be effective for Chicago's blacks.

King and his people still sensed victory, however, because of the dent they had been able to put into Daley's political hide. During the marches into Marquette Park, Gage Park and other bastions of blue collar workers, signs had appeared against Daley, signs that were raised by white men who had for decades provided the foundation for Daley's power. Those people, aligned with Chicago's blacks, could at the moment in history have turned over the Daley machine and voted in people who would work for and with them.

That was not to be. The Daley machine had long ago created a system by which those who voted were rewarded with real things. It was not uncommon for aldermen and ward organizers to pass around chickens, wine and cigarettes on voting day. The people who lived in the slums understood these goods. They could eat their payoff, or drink it or smoke it. It was a simple means of gaining favor, and even if it occurred once every two years, or in some cases once a year, the poor of Chicago did not forget.

Martin Luther King and his people did not give the poor blacks of Chicago chickens. Instead, they proposed an abstract reward—freedom and control of one's own political destiny. The starving ghetto dweller understood the chickens better. It was essentially the same problem which the Government of the United States has run into time and again in its foreign policy. As this country has struggled to battle Communism throughout the world, we have managed to walk into underdeveloped countries offering typewriters and freedom. You don't talk freedom to a man whose children are starving and whose apartment is infested with rats. His ability to think beyond the momentary problems of survival is limited, if not altogether non-existent.

So King found himself battling a machine that threw bones to its people. King had none to throw. The only strategy left was to raise his sword and swear to do battle. This King did not do.

During the fall of 1966, after the summer of marches and the "victory" over the open housing question, King came out with a statement that he was not intending to destroy Richard Daley and his machine. Instead, he said, he would be starting a voter registration drive in Chicago with the intention of politicizing the blacks and using the polls to create change.

In the minds of the black militants, and the more active members of the movement, King's statement was a retreat. They had felt that they had the momentum against Daley, that Daley was running scared. They felt, and probably rightfully so, that there was no system within which the blacks of Chicago could work. Daley controlled it all, and whatever victories would come would have to come from direct confrontation and by continually pushing Daley against the wall. Even the weak housing agreement, they said, had come only after the marches through white neighborhoods and the threatened march through Chicago. Sitting down and talking with Daley had never worked. Forcing him into the corner where political defeat lingered above his kingpin head had.

King began his voter registration drive, convinced that the Chicago blacks had seen the light and now would follow him and his troops to the polls to change things for the better. What King did not realize was that the system had deadened the sensibilities of the ghetto blacks to the point that nothing short of real, affirmative action could awaken them. Punching out ballots was meaningless to the people who had spent their lives trying to survive the ghetto. The only thing they understood about their city was that on voting days, and more likely Christmas time, their alderman would come around bearing dinner. King's drive was not strong enough to offset the bait of Daley's machine.

The voting drive during 1966 and early into 1967 was a dismal failure. King's staff became despondent over the lack of enthusiasm and awareness within the city's blacks. Even though Jesse Jackson had brought together Chicago's black ministers for King's initial plunge into Chicago, those same ministers were not bickering among themselves. The strength had dissipated. King found himself crying out for social justice and freedom to a deaf audience.

The movement also came up against another huge obstacle known as the welfare state. Local offices of the state welfare agencies within Chicago were controlled and monitored by the local politicians. A black man or woman who fed his or her family from the monies collected from the welfare state was hard pressed to forego that security. To go against the local machine representatives, and thus Daley himself, was an act tantamount to committing welfare suicide. Since King had not declared open war on Daley, he became just another weakened voice trying to do battle with the Chicago machine. People had lost the hope that one day, if they sacrificed all, they would be able to march as one with King onto the steps of city hall and take over the city.

Another little phenomenon which has existed in Chicago for many decades made the voter registration drive impossible from the beginning. This phenomenon became apparent and received much publicity during the Kennedy election to the Presidency in 1960. Daley had at the time promised to deliver Cook County to the Democratic candidate, a promise that had long ago been kept time and time again, and a promise that throughout the years would keep the federal hounds off the mayor's back and allow him to develop and hone his machine without interference.

The scandal broke when the election returns were filed, and experts began to suspect foul play in Cook County. The margin of victory was so small for Kennedy that the county could have been pivotal. Nixon's people declared foul play, asked for a recount, then withdrew their request. Apparently, no one was ready to go up against the Daley machine. Yet the rumors have persisted throughout the years. As in that election, Daley has delivered the votes when they were needed. Techniques such as dual registration, using his own foot soldiers to vote for the illiterate, and even having dead men cast their ballots are methods that have long been associated with Daley's voter machine. Plus there is the control which Daley and his people exert over the voter himself. Whether the ballot in Chicago is a matter of Daley record, or remains a private matter between the voter and his ballot is a question which had been raised over and over again. The local voter seemed to think that everyone within the local precinct would know how he voted, and the reactions of the local politicians and aldermen to a "wrong" vote would usually confirm his worst fears. Whether or not King and his people had run up against a pure violation of the Constitution—the non-secret ballot—no one ever knew. But many of the people they attempted to register certainly acted as if they had.

The elections approached, and the movement was bombing dramatically with its last ditch effort to gain some kind of political clout within Chicago. In April of 1967, the movement literally died as a voting power in Chicago when Daley was swept into office once again. It was Daley's fourth term, and he won it by collecting seventy-three percent of the votes cast. In the black precincts, Daley won by a margin of five-to-one. So, even after King and his forces had walked into Chicago and had seemed to disrupt the machine of Richard Daley, the king of Chicago emerged stronger than ever. The marches, the confrontations, the apparent victories all seemed for naught. Daley reigned again, even stronger than before.

Daley seized the opportunity with a clenched fist, the kind of powerful and direct response which King had failed to make when he had Daley on the run. Daley addressed the city in his inaugural speech and told his people that no longer would he tolerate the lack of law and order in his town. What he was saying was that King and his people would no longer have the "freedom" to violate the laws of Chicago by marching in its streets; Daley himself would no longer sit back and allow the blacks to disrupt the peaceful flow of his machine. The fourth term election of Richard Daley had convinced the mayor that he no longer needed the support of the movement to win. He realized, probably with a certain amount of glee, that Civil Rights was not an issue among *his* blacks that no matter what he did or how he treated King and his boys, *his* blacks would still react positively to his local machine and cast their ballots accordingly.

The election seemed to wipe out every step which King and his men had made. One of Daley's aides, an alderman named Thomas Keane, came out immediately after the election and informed the press that the housing agreement signed the summer before was, in fact, not a real agreement at all. Keane went on to explain that the agreement was nothing more than a series of goals and ideas which would be explored as time went on.

As Daley's politicos stood up one by one and denied the agreement supporting their boss in his new turn away from human rights, the blacks of Chicago did not react. They did not riot, nor did they call on Martin Luther King to don the shield and sword and go into battle. This was, after all, Chicago. Richard Daley, as always, was stating truth and reality as he saw fit.

The defeat in 1967 worked to begin splintering the movement. The workers and King himself left the city to return to the South and begin dealing again with the kind of politics they understood. Many of the aides, attempting to retain a sense of brotherhood with their fellow blacks in Chicago nevertheless let slip a feeling of animosity, almost disgust, towards the weak responding residents of the Chicago ghettos. The movement had come up against America's most powerful local machine and had lost. The test case had been a failure, and Martin Luther King's Southern Christian Leadership Conference would never quite recover. They had played ball in the "minor" leagues of the South and had won their share of games. Once they stepped into the huge stadium of the northern powerbrokers, they found themselves leaving town with their tail between their legs.

Even though many of the SCLC staffers began blaming one another and blaming Chicago's blacks, there was truthfully no one at fault. Martin Luther King had brought spirituality and non-violent demonstrations to a city which had as its legacy Al Capone and Richard Daley. King had sought to do battle with a machine that even presidential candidates would not buck. The North was truly a different country.

Through the nightmare that was 1966-67, Jesse Jackson watched and worked. His quick mind and quick perceptions did not miss what was happening to his hero. King had marched for open housing, then had sought to register the voters. He had failed. The Chicago machine, Jackson began to note, was tied too powerfully into the financial bloodline of the people to destroy through something as abstract as "equality."

As King and his troops left Chicago, they did not leave in total defeat. Jesse Jackson had provided one glimmer of hope with his Operation Breadbasket. Jackson had already shown King that he could bring together diverse interests, as he had done with the black ministers. During King's stay in Chicago, Jackson was proving with effectiveness that Breadbasket did provide some hope down the line.

Jesse Jackson had been given the economic arm of the SCLC in Chicago because he was a man not involved with local prejudices and in-house skirmishes. Jackson was young, energetic and full of fresh blood. When he spoke with a minister, it was not out of malice or jealousy, but out of his need to improve relations with his Operation Breadbasket. On Saturday mornings, Jackson had begun his weekly sermons. The crowds had been increasing, and people had begun paying attention. The foremost reason for Jackson's success was his ability to go right to the heart of the matter. That heart was money.

The abstractions had not worked, the pleas for spiritual enlightenment had failed, and even the political clout of the marches had not turned the tide of Chicago's treatment of blacks.

What Jesse Jackson discovered to be working was economic boycotts, a means of striking directly into the financial gut of those businesses who refused to hire blacks, or buy black products. Even as the SCLC pulled out, Jackson's boycotts were producing results. Blacks were being hired. The realization began to sink in that an effective stance against the chickens of the Machine on voting days was a good job year round. Jesse Jackson was giving the blacks of Chicago something real, something they could touch and feel—money in their pockets. He was circumventing the open housing issue entirely and concentrating only on bringing money into the ghetto. It would prove to be a goal that even Mayor Daley could understand and deal with. Money was the answer in Chicago, and Jesse Jackson was becoming a master of finance.

Overleaf: Jesse Jackson is shown at an early 1970s Civil Rights Movement rally with black activist Maggie Hathaway.

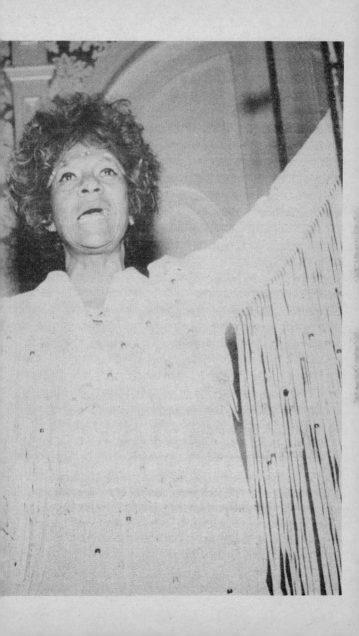

Los Angeles Mayor Tom Bradley, never a strong supporter of Jesse Jackson in the early years, was one of the many black leaders who discouraged him from running for the presidency as a third ticket candidate in 1984, feeling that Jackson would pull votes away from Walter Mondale and assure the re-election of Ronald Reagan.

Chapter 4

A Leader Emerges

As Martin Luther King, Jr. did battle with Mayor Daley and his Chicago machine, Jesse Jackson worked on the sidelines developing clout with his Operation Breadbasket. The logic behind the economic arm of the SCLC rested with the fact that blacks in America contributed some six billion dollars to the national economy through their purchasing power. Jackson, as well as King, saw that this huge influx into the economy could be used against the system which oppressed blacks to force concessions that would allow them to rise within the social and financial spectrum. Thus was born the idea of Operation Breadbasket, a simple and straight-forward means of eliciting demands from the white business establishment based on the threat of economic boycott. "Don't give our people what they need," Breadbasket said, "and all the blacks will stop using your products."

As Jesse Jackson explained it: "We are the margin of profit of every major item produced in America from General Motors cars on down to Kellogg's Corn Flakes." Jackson, in his usual blunt and audacious style went on to add that, "If we've got his margin of profit, we've got his genitals."

Jackson began to realize how much power he held in being able to bring people together during 1966 when he organized the local ministers in Chicago to support the arrival of Dr. King. It was a gigantic step forward to be able to coalesce these divided factions into one unit of action. Jackson learned what the SCLC had been practicing for years, that if you get the preachers behind you, the flocks will follow. Although this technique failed miserably in the voter registration drive which King launched in Chicago, it would work with Jesse Jackson's Breadbasket boycotts.

The structure of the boycott was simple. Jackson would get together with local preachers and decide on a target business in their neighborhood. They would then investigate and find out how many blacks were working for that particular company, and how many black products that company used. The clergymen and Jackson would then draw up a list of demands; how many blacks should be hired, how many black products should be used, and where some of the capital should be put, namely black owned banks. These demands would be sent to the business.

If the owners of the business told Jackson to take his demands and jump into Lake Michigan, then Jackson would tell his preachers to inform their flocks that that business was off-limits until the demands had been met. Boycott through the churches was the name of this game, and Jackson and his ministers played it well.

The first business to feel the power of Operation Breadbasket was a dairy named Country Delight, Inc. When approached by Jackson, Country Delight refused to show him their records. Disclosure was out of the question. In one hundred churches on Chicago's Southside the following Sunday, the call went out from the mouths of one hundred preachers: Do not do business with Country Delight. It took Country Delight only three days to feel the power of the black consumer on the Southside. Country Delight came to the bargaining table with an offer of forty-four new and upgraded jobs for blacks. The first test of Breadbasket's boycott had been a rousing success.

Jackson and his group then "hit" a Chicago grocery chain called High-Low Foods. The boycott lasted for ten days, and finally High-Low offered Jackson and Breadbasket one-hundred-eighty-four new jobs for blacks in its fifty-four stores. The jobs ranged from managers down to janitors, but they were jobs which had not been there previously.

One boycott which became famous for pointing out the conditions under which blacks existed in the ghettos was the action taken by Jackson against a market chain known as The Red Rooster, Inc.

Red Rooster Markets had long been criticized in Chicago

for their extreme health violations. They had been on the edge of scandal more than once, with accusations of having paid off health inspectors in order to shelve products which ranged from rancid meat to spoiled milk. The Red Rooster chain catered to the Southside blacks. Their dangerously rancid food and the conditions within the market continued to be tolerated. Had they been in a white neighborhood, they would have been shut down years before.

However, the Red Rooster chain stayed in business, working like a slum landlord of food. They would extend credit where other markets would not, they would lower their prices for meat that was inedible, and they would generally exploit their black neighbors without mercy.

Operation Breadbasket hit the Red Rooster, bringing to attention the terrible health conditions of the markets. Not only would the chain have to agree to hire blacks, but they would also have to clean their stores and completely renovate their operation. The boycott against Red Rooster resulted in the entire chain going out of business and permanently closing its doors. The owner called Jackson a "liar," while others claimed that Jackson was practicing nothing less than extortion. Those who had seen the markets agreed that for the health and well-being of Chicago's blacks, it was all for the best that the stores had disappeared from the streets.

The boycott, which brought Jackson and his Operation Breadbasket into the national limelight, however, was the sixteen-week boycott against the A&P Corporation which owned some forty stores in Chicago's black neighborhoods. The huge chain held out as long as it could, but Jackson stood firm. Finally, the company gave in. They agreed to hire two-hundred-sixty-eight blacks as managers, executives and workers. More important than that, A&P agreed to stock black products on its shelves. Grove Fresh orange juice, Mumbo Barbecue Sauce, Staff of Life bread, Joe Louis Milk and King Solomon spray deodorant were but a few of the total of twenty-five products owned and produced by blacks which the chain agreed to stock. Not only did they agree to stock them, they promised to display them in prominent places.

The A&P boycott resulted in one more victory. The chain promised to use black services, such as janitorial work, pest extermination and garbage collection. As Jackson said later, "We have a monopoly on rats in the ghetto, and we're going to have a monopoly on killing them."

Jackson's vision of economic wealth within the ghetto was not just confined to more jobs for blacks. As Operation Breadbasket became more successful, Jackson persuaded neighborhood businesses to do their banking exclusively with black-owned banks. In two banks located in Chicago's black neighborhoods, combined assets rose from $5 million to $22 million within a very short period of time. Along with keeping the banks rolling, Jackson pressed for all building contracts and services to be given to black businesses. In effect, Jackson was creating a spiral of economic growth situated within the black community. The consumers would buy black products, creating jobs for blacks in those companies which produced them, and the money that these businesses made would go into black banks where loans for new businesses were more accesible to the black businessman.

Operation Breadbasket was succeeding on a level where the SCLC and other groups had failed. Jackson had skirted right by the issues and gone directly to the economic cause. It appeared that he was becoming extremely successful.

Jackson extended his operation into other cities during this period. Los Angeles, Milwaukee, Brooklyn, Houston and Cleveland were but a few cities to receive new chapters of Operation Breadbasket. None was as successful as that which blossomed in Chicago.

In Cleveland, Operation Breadbasket tried its hand in the political arena. In the municipal election of 1969, Mayor Carl Stokes was vying for re-election. The blacks in Cleveland feared police harassment at the polls as a means of insuring that Stokes would not be re-elected. It was assumed that the majority of voters would arrive at the polls after work, sometimes in the late afternoon and early evening. Operation Breadbasket interceded with troops from Chicago plus over 600 young gang members. Jackson instructed them to go through the black neighborhoods as dawn broke over Cleveland and to make so much noise that the sleeping voters would be awakened. The blacks were then encouraged to hit the polls prior to work, instead of waiting until they finished their work day. The results were successful, Carl Stokes was elected to another term, and there was little, if any, harassment of the black voters at the voting booths that day.

The economic success of Operation Breadbasket during those early years was a direct result of effective action, and of Jesse Jackson's own personal brand of charisma and charm. In Chicago, Jackson was quickly becoming a super-hero.

When Jackson arrived in Chicago to study theology, he began working with Martin Luther King and the SCLC. Jackson's ability to give a speech and charm a crowd pulled him further and further away from the seminary. In 1969, Jackson was ordained after having dropped out of the seminary to devote himself full time to the SCLC and its Operation Breadbasket. It was obvious to those around him that Jesse Jackson was moving upwards, that he was an emerging leader.

By 1967, Jackson had his own pulpit from which to speak. In his offices on the Southside, Jackson began spreading his influence throughout Chicago, but the big moment came every Saturday morning where the spiritual bonds of Operation Breadbasket were originally secured and stayed tied throughout the following years. In an old auditorium on Chicago's Southside, Jesse Jackson began speaking on a regular basis every Saturday morning to hundreds and thousands of fans. This show, a combination revival, strategy meeting and ghetto social, became the foundation from which Jackson began to emerge.

The meetings began at nine o'clock in the morning, and lasted for three hours. One hour and a half was carried by local radio. Since the beginning, the network of national stations picked up the broadcasts and had increased so that almost everywhere in the country the Saturday morning meetings were heard.

From these Saturday morning revivals came the now famous cry of Jesse Jackson: "I am somebody." Like a chorus in a revival tent in the deep South, the audience at these meetings would chant with Jesse, raising to a fevered pitch the slogan that the individual black man is a meaningful human being.

Along with drawing big crowds and getting the attention of the media, the Saturday morning meetings of Operation Breadbasket brought to the forefront, once and for all, Jesse Jackson's talent as a preacher. Many people began to see that he was a perfect link between the old fashioned, moralistic preacher and the new wave black man who sought change through direct action. Jackson oftentimes was accused of emulating Martin Luther King, especially during the months following King's assassination. Those who listened carefully, however, understood that Jesse was playing the role of the Southern preacher, using his voice like a musical instrument to affect the emotions of the people who listened.

This combination of emotional oration and effective action separated Jesse Jackson from the other leaders of the movement during the late sixties. Jackson seemed to be a bridge, a much needed link between the younger and older generation.

Even in his style of dress, Jesse Jackson began winning fans who were young enough and fired with enough energy to make a difference. Jackson chose to dress casually, wearing Levis, boots and open shirts. The suits and slender ties of the Kings and Abernathys were out for Jackson. He was beginning to speak to the young folks, and they were listening.

Jackson's emergence through the SCLC, and his close association with King, gave the young leader a hold on the movement that no one else possessed. He was considered "legitimate" by the press because he had marched with King. He was not feared as a nothing-to-lose radical who would opt for bloodshed and violence over reasonable solution. Yet Jackson's style appealed to radical elements. They saw in him a modern black man, a lean and hungry doer who would make changes, who would live in the style of the seventies. The young seemed to turn to Jackson quickly, especially after King's death in Memphis.

In 1968, the movement was bogged down in its own image. King was gone, and everyone knew that no one would ever replace him. Martin Luther King had been a special kind of man, and people sensed that his appearance on earth was something akin to a miracle. He would be sorely missed, and he would not be replaced.

Jesse Jackson rose from the chaos as a figure who worshipped Dr. King and his ideals, making no attempt to duplicate his style, at least not in the manner in which he dressed and presented himself to the public. While Ralph Abernathy and the survivors of King's entourage appeared in public mournful and despondent, dressing in the same old suits and saying the same things, Jesse Jackson came on like a new, bright light. He was not so far from King as to do disservice to the memory of the great man, but at the same time Jackson was obviously different, a new breed of black cat ready to make his move.

In the Saturday morning meeting, this new black cat begn to capture the imagination and the energy of blacks throughout the country. Jackson's message was basically the same as King's, except one ingredient remained as a departure. King had always spoken of the dignity of the human spirit, and of the black man's struggle as a unified entity and a mass. He had brought the black people to gether under the banner of their racial identity. Once they had been grouped as such, Jesse Jackson dared them to take another step.

"I am somebody," the call and anthem of the Saturday morning meetings, became a challenge to the blacks in the audience to go further than identifying themselves as black men and women, but to stand up and face the world as individuals. What Jackson seemed to be saying was "Look at me, I am a beautiful black cat who is somebody. I am foremost and always me."

Tom Wolfe, the writer, called the seventies the "Me Generation." He cited examples of people retreating into themselves, looking for their spiritual awakening, becoming a generation of selfish creatures dealing only with the problems of self rather than with the problems of the world around them. Political philosophy has always meandered between the world view and the selfish interest point of view as to which is the most productive for society as a whole. Martin Luther King strode across the country as an example of a man who had denied "self." Whenever an item broke about King doing something as an individual, instead of as an egoless representative of his race, the headlines would jump. For his time and place, King was perfect. He was able to gather the black man together, to make him look at his world and his place in it without feeling the incredible frustration and hopelessness of his ego. King was able to get the black man to understand that it wasn't just himself, but that it was all of his black brothers and sisters who were suffering.

Jesse Jackson was then able to make the black man feel just a little selfish once again. He was able to make the black man separate himself from his race for a moment and look at himself as a human being again, not just as an oppressed black man.

It is human nature for the individual to be selfish. A man with a wife and children looks to the care and feeding of his own brood before he will sacrifice to a greater cause. That is precisely why King's voter registration drive in Chicago failed. King was asking local blacks to give up what little security, even though it was a sham, that they felt they had with the Daly political machine. Jesse Jackson was not asking his people to surrender security. He was asking them merely not to buy certain products and to begin regarding themselves as successes. He was asking them to begin looking at themselves as winners, as fighters within the ring of capitalism, as men and women who had the brains, determination and guts to play the game along with the white man.

Jesse Jackson was not denying the world to his people. Instead, he was trying to teach them how to deal with it effectively.

With Jackson's Operation Breadbasket creating jobs and money within the black community, and his Saturday morning speeches tying a spiritual knot, the two ends of the movement spectrum were being brought together. Real benefits in the form of money were being felt within the community, and the people were beginning to look up to a man who acted and spoke like he lived in the real urban world of the seventies.

The eventual split between Jesse Jackson and his parent organization, the SCLC, was only a matter of time. Jackson was moving too fast for the leaderless SCLC, and his feud with Ralph Abernathy was splitting allegiances all the way down the line. The movement was beginning to separate and drift into two factions—the North and the South.

The split had begun back in 1966, when Jackson raised the ire of the SCLC staffers with his audacious personality and his ability to shove himself into the headlines. Resentment flared within the hierarchy of the SCLC because of Jackson. He seemed to be an upstart, a Johnny-come-lately who was grabbing all the attention but who had not paid his dues. Staffers complained about him, but they were forced to tolerate him. One reason was that Jackson was effective. No one could deny the success he had begun having with Operation Breadbasket. No one could deny his ability to organize. It was also evident that Jackson was a charismatic human being, capable of generating news and adding energy to the movement.

The other reason that Jesse Jackson was accepted was that Dr. King seemed to like him. Like all great leaders, King was able to incorporate and work with diverse personalities and mentalities. In Jesse Jackson, King obviously saw a young man who was different than the other men on his staff. He most likely recognized in Jackson a shift into the future. Younger than any of his staff, Jackson was of a different breed. By assigning him to Chicago's Operation Breadbasket, it seemed as though King had given Jackson the rope and leverage he needed to see what he could do.

So Jackson stayed within the ranks of the SCLC, working almost as an orbiting energy, independent and self starting, constantly creating dissention within the ranks by making unauthorized statements on his own. King saw that he was effective and would not risk a break with this valuable young worker. The movement was too important for that, and King was too great a man to attempt to destroy the energy and burning desire of a committed man like Jesse Jackson.

When Martin Luther King, Jr. slumped onto the second floor balcony of the Lorraine Motel that April night in 1968, it was not only a man that fell, but also a certain, undefinable spirit. That spirit had been the genius of Dr. King, a spirit that would not be as strong ever again.

In the name and memory of that spirit, however, Jesse Jackson and the SCLC attempted to remain allied, at least to the general public. But once again, resentment towards Jackson ran high in the councils of the SCLC. Abernathy, Andy Young and others were irate over Jackson's alleged media stunt of claiming that he was the last man to speak with King, and that he wore a sweater stained with the blood of the martyr. These men felt strongly that Jackson had taken advantage of a tragic situation with only one goal in mind—to further his own career.

Jackson ignored the cries of foul play and continued to build his Chicago organization through Operation Breadbasket. Over the next two years, Jackson's attitude toward the SCLC changed, and he was heard speaking of Abernathy in negative terms. Time Magazine quoted him as saying: "I never listen to that nigger." Other sources quoted Jackson as referring to Abernathy as a man who says and means all the right things but a man who was incompetent and incapable.

Abernathy, meanwhile, concentrated on carrying out

King's work in the deep South. The SCLC was still the most powerful civil rights organization in the country, and there was still work to be done.

It was also evident that on the surface, Jackson would not be making a direct assault at Abernathy's presidency. Abernathy seemed capable of taking whatever Jackson had to offer behind closed doors, so long as Jackson did not split the SCLC down the middle.

Jackson's drive to claim leadership of the black movement at this time was obvious to almost everyone. The national press heralded him as the heir apparent to King; and in 1970, a special issue of Time Magazine ran Jackson on its cover.

Jesse Jackson did not really make his move towards power in an overt manner until the first Black Expo in 1970. It was then that his ambition was clarified for everyone to see.

The Black Expo was a brainchild of the people at Operation Breadbasket, mostly an invention of Jesse Jackson. The idea was to gather together businessmen and tradesmen in a soulful, fun convention and exchange ideas, open accounts and stimulate black business. Jackson had become popular enough within the entertainment industry to call upon stars of the highest magnitude to perform for his Expo. The Jackson Five, Cannonball Adderly, Nancy Wilson and other popular entertainers gathered to perform spectacular shows once a night during the five-day trade show.

The first Black Expo was staged under the banner of the SCLC in conjunction with Operation Breadbasket. All proceeds for the trade show were to go to SCLC, and the various businesses which sponsored the show.

Expo '70 was a success. Black and white businessmen arrived from all over the country. Small businesses overnight became successes, and trade was increased and stimulated within the minority communities.

For Jackson, the show was a tremendous success. He was the center of attention. It became Jackson's show and not the baby of the SCLC. During the trade show's run, Jackson made sure that everyone knew exactly who he was by circulating thousands of copies of an article which had appeared in Playboy Magazine heralding Jackson as the next national leader of the Civil Rights Movement. This was at a time when Abernathy was president of the SCLC, and should have been in the position of being the national leader.

The following year, Operation Breadbasket staged another Black Expo, but this time, incorporated themselves under the name of Black Expo. Financially, this left the SCLC in the dark, without any claim to the profits of the venture. When the convention was over, this fact would lead to the final split between Jackson and the SCLC.

It was during the actual convention itself that it became evident the split had already taken place. The blackout of Ralph Abernathy was obvious and complete. During the trade show, speakers praised the past and current heroes of the black movement. Roy Wilkins, Martin Luther King, Jr., and Jesse Jackson were all spoken of in terms of being the leaders of the movement. Ralph Abernathy's name was not even mentioned.

In the auditorium where the speeches took place, huge portraits hung from the back wall. There were pictures

89

of King, Whitney Young and Jesse Jackson again. Missing was a portrait of Ralph Abernathy. The snub was not taken lightly by Abernathy, nor by the people at the SCLC.

The SCLC and Abernathy investigated the gate and entertainment receipts of the Expo Trade Fair and found a wide discrepancy between the announced attendance and the amount of money collected by the SCLC. No one even hinted that Jackson had embezzled funds. Nevertheless, Abernathy suspended Jackson for sixty days because of his inability to handle the finances of the Black Expo.

What Abernathy did not know at the time was that Black Expo had already severed its ties with the SCLC and had incorporated itself independent of the parent group. Abernathy was surprised and embarrassed when he discovered this fact, and instantly demanded a full investigation into the financial operation of the black trade show .

Jackson was infuriated by Abernathy's investigation. Finally, Jackson and Abernathy met to straighten out the mess. Jackson explained that the black businessmen had wanted Black Expo incorporated in order to protect their liabilities. The maneuver was entirely legal. The only question was, why hadn't Abernathy been informed of the change?

Jackson answered with a shrug, saying that he had sent a memo to SCLC's headquarters, but that the organization had never been "memo conscious."

The investigation by Abernathy and the ensuing confrontation and suspension convinced Jackson that it was time to break the umbilical cord. He decided to resign from the SCLC and attempt to start his own human rights organization.

In a jam-packed auditorium on Chicago's Southside, Jesse Jackson spoke emotionally about his life with the SCLC. Then he told his cheering followers that he would turn over Operation Breadbasket and all of its assets to the SCLC. When Jackson resigned from the SCLC, he told his throng of admirers that: "I love the organization I grew up with. But I need air. I got to grow."

The break came around the beginning of December in 1971. Jackson was literally without a home, with no parent organization to support him. There were many who thought he had made a mistake, that he had jumped too soon. But Jesse Jackson rarely jumps too soon into anything. He always seems to know what his moves will entail before making them.

When Jackson resigned his post with Operation Breadbasket, he took his entire thirty-five man staff with him. Also included in the number of men and women who jumped ship were twenty-five out of thirty board members of Operation Breadbasket. These people were obviously ready to follow their leader, not the company.

Along with the members who made the move with Jackson, waiting in the wings were a number of fund-raisers, businessmen and entertainers ready and quite able to help Jackson raise whatever funds would be necessary to begin his own organization. Among them were Manhattan borough president Percy Sutton; Mayor Richard Hatcher of Gary, Indiana; popular singer Aretha Franklin; former all-time great fullback of the Cleveland Browns turned actor, Jim Brown; and powerful actor Ossie Davis. There were more waiting for Jesse Jackson: Hugh Hefner, publisher of Playboy Magazine which had called Jack son the "heir apparent" to Martin Luther King, hundreds of show business personalities who had been fans of the flamboyant, attractive Jackson for years.

Most important to Jackson was his machine, a machine that would eventually do battle with Mayor Daley over the seating at the 1972 Democratic Convention. This machine consisted of those businessmen, both black and white, whom Jackson had helped to become millionaires. To them, Jackson was not so much a spiritual leader as he was a pragmatic businessman. These people were all ready to help Jackson begin a thrust of his own.

As Christmas approached, Jesse Jackson finally announced his plans for a new organization. Three thousand people jammed into the Metropolitan Theater on Chicago's Southside to listen to the announcement of a birth. On the sidewalks outside, thousands stood in the December chill and listened over loudspeakers. Jesse Jackson, speaking from the stage with dramatic lighting and a huge portrait of Martin Luther King, Jr., announced that on Christmas Day of 1971, operation PUSH would be officially born.

People United to Save Humanity, operation PUSH, in the words of its founder, it was a "rainbow coalition" of blacks and whites gathered together to "push for a greater share of economic and political power for all poor people in America in the spirit of Dr. Martin Luther King, Jr."

The break between Jackson and the SCLC was final, Jackson promised to take nothing from Breadbasket. Abernathy said that he would continue the program, both in the South and North. Most importantly, however, Jesse

Jackson was finally on his own.

The goal of PUSH was very much the same as Bread-basket had been under Jackson's leadership. The stress would be on economic growth of the black man and his community. The big difference with PUSH would be its focusing on politics as well. Jackson believed that if he could get the politicians aligned with his programs, then legislation could be passed that would ease the problems of black economic growth.

The first year of PUSH's operation would cost Jackson and his people nearly half a million dollars, but the support was tremendous. The businessmen, the entertainers and everyone who had been following Jackson lent their support.

Two years after the announcement of PUSH, Jesse Jackson toured the nation, mobilizing a demonstration in Memphis to commemorate the sixth anniversary of Martin Luther King's death. Within two years PUSH had produced satellites throughout the country, and Jackson had been able to bring together hundreds of thousands of workers to support his economic program.

In an article written in Ebony, Jackson spoke about the first two years of PUSH. He called the demonstration in Memphis a rousing confirmation of Martin Luther King's goal to "save the worker." Jackson then outlined the program that was PUSH: "The goal of our movement at this point in history is to secure jobs for those already working but not making a livable wage organized. That has to be the three-pronged thrust of our Civil Economics Movement."

In two years, Jesse Jackson had changed the dialogue

and calling card of the movement. It was now a "civil economic movement," and not a civil rights movement. Jackson had finally thrust himself into the guts of the issue, and was speaking to people directly about their jobs and welfare. Although still a preacher, and a dramatically successful one, Jackson had becoming primarily a money-changer, a man who generated work, created "new" money and tried to play one end against the other to keep the black economy moving. PUSH had become Jackson's weapon against black injustice. It had also become a powerful machine, an economic entity to be reckoned with.

When PUSH was born in 1971, it was the birth of a new kind of movement. More like a huge corporation than a movement, it was structured to deal with money as a means of solving the problems of inequality and racial injustice. PUSH, like Jesse Jackson himself, seemed to be in step with its own time and history.

Chapter 5

Jesse's Battles With Mayor Daley

In May of 1968, only one month after the assassination of Martin Luther King, thousands of poor people from across the country converged upon the nation's capital in an attempt to dramatize the plight of the poor. They came from every corner of the country, bringing with them their belongings—tents, sleeping bags, cooking stoves and other materials which would allow them to camp in an area near the capital known as Resurrection City.

The Poor People's March had been an idea born from the mind of Martin Luther King during one of his side trips into the rural South. He had felt at the time that by expanding the consciousness of the nation outwards, beyond the black issue and into the issue of poverty as it existed among all peoples, he would be able to generate greater enthusiasm and support.

The assassination of Dr. King left the huge undertaking without a leader. Ralph Abernathy took over, and was held responsible for what would later be termed a "fiasco."

When the throngs gathered in Washington, D.C., they were greeted by a Mother Nature that obviously did not support the poor. The rains came, flooding the grounds on which the people had erected their temporary city. Chaos reigned throughout the days of the demonstration. Within Resurrection City itself, there was trouble. Assaults, theft and rape occurred among the people, and there was very little policing from within the city itself. As the world watched, the nation's poor demonstrated that they were like other people, that they were unable to remain saintly under unsaintly conditions.

Ralph Abernathy lost control. The chaos was growing, and Abernathy left the city to stay in a motel blocks away. The situation was becoming a disaster.

Jesse Jackson arrived from Chicago, and Abernathy, in a supposedly joking manner, appointed Jackson mayor of Resurreciton City. Jackson took the appointment seriously. He addressed the huge, chaotic crowd and told them to pull themselves together. In his speech, Jackson used the techniques which he often incorporated when dealing with fellow blacks, one in which he would set himself up as a "badder ass" than anyone else in the crowd. The people responded to Jackson, especially the younger ones, and soon Jackson had brought some control and order to what had been a disintegrating situation.

Jackson stayed around a few more days, then claimed illness and returned to Chicago with a stopover in Los Angeles to appear on a nationally broadcast television show.

Ralph Abernathy stayed with the people in Resurrection City and wound up taking all the heat for what had become a disastrous demonstration. Jesse Jackson had swept in and out quickly enough to avoid the bad publicity, appearing only as a hero who had managed to bring order where once there had been chaos.

What this incident showed was that Jesse Jackson was now moving on his own. With the death of Dr. King, he was not responding to the dictates of the SCLC, nor was he attempting to work in complete unison with Abernathy. If Dr. King had been alive, it is highly possible that Jackson would have assumed another role. In his absence, Jackson was showing that his responsibility to the SCLC was quickly coming to an end, at least in his own mind.

What this also meant was that Jesse Jackson would have to return to Chicago and do battle with Mayor Richard Daley on his own. It would no longer be a dual front, a combination of Jackson's group within the city and Abernathy's Southern SCLC as had been the case during Dr. King's marches through the city. The murder of Dr. King had destroyed the umbilical cord, and even though it would take three years for Jackson to officially resign from the SCLC, the Poor People's Campaign demonstrated that a large schism already existed.

What lay ahead for Jesse Jackson in Chicago, no one at the time could predict. The nation had watched as the most powerful and charismatic leader of black people in history had played the game with the mayor and lost. They had watched as Dr. King left the city in defeat, returning to the South where he understood the rules and the machines.

Now, the nation watched as a young, brash leader, after making the newly crowned president of the SCLC look impotent and somewhat foolish, returned to do battle on his own with the powerful Daley. It would be Jackson's baptism into politics, doing battle with a machine that no one had yet been able to conquer.

Jesse Jackson was smart, and he was not as fully committed to the issues that had forced Dr. King into defeat. Although Jackson wanted the same things as King, he was not as confined to the techniques that Dr. King had been.

Jesse Jackson began fighting the Daley machine by not fighting it at all. The issues which had defeated King—open housing being the most sensitive and in the end, the most lethal—Jackson would completely avoid. He would attempt to skirt Daley and his boys, doing a delicate end around sweep until the time was right to confront the mayor directly. This was Jackson's genius in dealing with northern politics.

In 1969, Jesse Jackson realized that in order to build and preserve his economic victories within the city of Chicago, he would have to somehow begin developing political clout. The license boards, the health boards, the city inspectors—all those people who were in Daley's back pocket—who determined who built what and where in Chicago, had to be dealt with. The machine was powerful. Business and politics in Chicago could not be separated.

Chicago as Jackson found it in 1969 was a closed city. Every politician, ward alderman, and precinct captain was in Daley's pocket. Daley himself was in a disturbed mood. Dr. King had come to his city and shown the nation that Chicago was not the black man's paradise that Daley had claimed it to be. Riots, marches and demonstrations had brought Chicago into the nation's eye as a city in which the race problem was festering.

As King brought the attention of the media to Chicago, people started putting figures together regarding that city's relationship to its black population. Some of the findings were startling. The record of the Chicago police department, for instance, and its kill rate of blacks versus whites was incredible. Out of all the deaths at the hands of cops, seventy-five percent were blacks. On the Southside of Chicago, police brutality was a fact of life.

The lifestyle of the blacks in Chicago had not been changed perceptively since Dr. King had taken the rundown, rat-infested apartment on the Southside to demonstrate the living conditions of the city's poor. The slums were intolerable, filled with garbage on the streets, inadequate heating and cooling, and conditions which under normal city governments would have been declared unlivable by health officials. But once again, the men who reported to the Mayor and signed the papers were on Daley's payroll, the inspectors having gotten their jobs as a result of Daley's favoritism.

The problems of school integration were also tremendous in Chicago. According to surveys taken at the time, Chicago had the worst record of segregation of any major city in the North. Even when Dr. King came to Chicago and prompted the ''resignation'' of Superintendent Willis, the situation within the schools had not changed much. Black kids were stuffed into tiny classrooms and into schools that were ill-suited to proper education.

Jesse Jackson had won victories with his economic assault on the black community, filtering money into the ghetto through the machinations of his Operation Breadbasket. Mayor Daley had stayed away from the boycotts, allowing Jackson to fight his own battles with the supermarket chains and independent businesses. When Daley desired to align the blacks on his side, he would move them against a Republican candidate. For once, the blacks and Daley would move together under a harmonious flag, but when it came down to real issues of the street, like housing, food and education, Mayor Daley would not budge. His gamesmanship had defeated Dr. King, and Jesse Jackson would find playing in Chicago by Daley's rules just as tough.

Jackson began his campaign within the city's body politic by attacking with two different weapons, weapons which Dr. King really did not have at his disposal. First, there was Jackson's economic block—those businessmen who had profited under Jackson's Operation Breadbasket; and secondly, there was Jackson's ability to move on the fringes of the major issues. Dr. King had been committed to those issues. Jackson was not. Therein lay a huge difference between the two men and their walk through Chicago politics.

Powerful moral issues are oftentimes the best way to begin a campaign. By choosing an issue which no one can really refute, at least in principal, you have the support of your enemy on paper if not in action. One year after the Poor People's campaign, Jesse Jackson chose the issue of hunger as his battle cry. On May 14, 1969, Jackson took two thousand people to the state capital in Springfield, Illinois, to march and protest against all hunger and malnutrition in the state.

Jackson addressed the elected public servants in Springfield that day, calling for Illinois to be declared a disaster area because of the hunger and starvation evident within the state. Jackson also called for a ban on slums, for a federal and state program for emergency job training programs in order to get blacks off welfare. The program, Jackson felt at the time, was soft enough in terms of hard political ramifications to get through the state assembly. Also, Jackson felt that by leaving Chicago and the environs of Cook County—he was skirting the Daley machine.

He was wrong. The web of power, with Chicago at its core, did extend throughout the state and into the Capitol dome. Without Daley's go ahead, these men, many of whom owed their positions to direct influence from the Daley machine, would not budge. The list of demands as presented by Jackson was soundly defeated.

Jackson was able to pull victory from the clutches of defeat, however, through a brilliant speech which he made to the state assembly shortly after the defeat of his proposals. The speech concerned the proposed cutback on Governor Richard Ogilvie's budget which would have cut welfare payments by thirty percent. Jackson packed the gallery of the assembly with housewives, young black gang members and movement people. He made an impassioned, hard hitting plea to reject the budget cut. The assembly responded and voted it down.

There are those, however, who claim that Jackson's victory within the assembly was a staged affair. Barbara Reynolds in her excellent biography on Jackson, claims that Ogilvie had actually persuaded the legislator who introduced the cutback to withdraw his budget directive a day before Jackson's speech. According to Miss Reynolds, this was done as a return favor to Jackson by Ogilvie for Jackson's support of him during the 1968 gubernatorial race. By staging the event, and allowing Jackson to come off as a hero to the poor by doing battle with the legislature, Jackson would never again carry the stigma of selling out to higher business interests. He would always be able to cite the battle at Springfield as evidence of his continuing and heroic dedication to the poor.

In her book, Miss Reynolds seems to feel that this is evidence of Jackson's cynical manipulation of events. What she seems to miss, however, is the point that Jackson did get the budget cut rescinded. By picking up an I.O.U. from the governor, Jackson was able to stop what would have become a disastrous budget cut for the poor people of Illinois, even if the ultimate victory was staged.

Was it harmful? Consider the results: by gleaning headlines and publicity, Jackson was able to publicize the plight of the welfare recipients, he was also able to marshall forces against the danger of the assembly and state legislature which appeared on the verge of slapping the poor directly in the face. Had it been merely a back-room agreement between Jackson and Ogilvie to get the budget cut withdrawn, no one would have known about it. It seems that the effect of the event was good for everyone. The dangers were publicized, Jackson gained more power with his people, and the budget cutback was stopped.

As a result of his battle and victory with the assembly, Jackson was able to bring together eleven black legislators and put them into his camp. These men were still products of Daley's machine, but that, even in the legislature—staged or not—opened a door in the minds of many people. It was beginning to appear that some victories could be won in the face of the machine. Through dramatic speech, forceful demonstration and the growing clout of Jesse Jackson, there seemed to be a camp growing to which people would be able to align themselves.

In June of 1969, Jesse Jackson regrouped his people and began a hunger march across the state. They ended their march in Springfield, and this time, the result was a hunger bill under which 5.4 million dollars was added to the federal subsidy program—money that was used to provide a free lunch during school to all children who were hungry. Hundreds of thousands of kids benefited.

In March of 1970, Jackson took his hunger campaign into the city of Chicago itself. With city elections coming up, it was felt that Jackson and his crusade would be able to exert some leverage against Daley and his machine.

Jackson was correct in thinking that his marches and demonstrations against hunger would begin to rile the mayor. Previously, Daley had denied the existence of hunger in Chicago. He had uttered such pronouncements as: "God forbid there are hungry people in Chicago," promising that if, indeed, he and his people could find one starving child, they would do everything within their power to make sure that the child had food on the table. Daley's health officials, after what they termed an "intensive investigation," also came back to city hall with the verdict that there was no hunger in Chicago.

Jackson began using the techniques developed by Dr. King and the movement to bring the situation to national attention. Even as the mayor was denying the existence of hungry people in his town, Jackson and his people were walking the streets of Chicago's Southside. Reporters followed them and took notes. Articles began appearing stating such glaring statistics such as: for every thousand babies in Chicago's Southside, forty-five would die of malnutrition and poor medical care before they reached two weeks of age. The people, themselves, began stepping forth with tales of horror. The press began running accounts of children eating dirt, of mothers feeding a family of five on a head of lettuce, of school children going two full days without eating a bite of food.

Jackson at this time implemented a direct feeding program through Operation Breadbasket. The Daley machine had used food throughout its history to gain the vote of the local citizens. On election day, those running for office would appear at the polling booths with a turkey or a ham, and the grateful voters would cast their ballot for the man who had fed them, even if that feeding occurred only every election day. Jackson understood the psychology and hoped that by using Daley's methods of food in the mouth—a vote on the ballet, he would be able to awaken the blacks to mark their votes for people who would seriously make an effort to help them.

The crusade through the Southside of Chicago began

working. The national media began paying attention, and the stories, too horrible and candid to be faked, began leaking out. Daley, never one to let an opportunity slide by, exclaimed his shock at the discovery that there were actually hungry people in his city. Attempting to steal Jackson's thunder as he'd done with Dr. King on the housing issue, Daley proclaimed an all out war against hunger in Chicago.

Just prior to the city elections, a council meeting was addressed by Jesse Jackson in which Jackson presented the city of Chicago with a proposal calling for $35 million to abolish hunger in that city. The council examined the proposal, then shuffled it off into committee. This was a major defeat for Jackson and his campaign.

According to sources, however, Jackson met with Richard Daley and settled on a compromise. The demands would be presented in open debate after the city elections if Jackson would call off his hounds during the elections. Daley was losing ground in some of his wars, and some of his hand-picked men were hanging precariously on the edge of defeat as a result of the hunger problem. Daley wanted to make sure his men got into office first. Then he would begin arbitration in open forum on the hunger issue.

Jesse Jackson learned the hard way the machinations of Daley's mind. It should have been evident after watching the downhill slide of Martin Luther King that Mayor Daley was not to be trusted with promises of future concessions. The compromise between Jackson and Daley irritated many observers of the scene in Chicago, and for good reason.

Once the elections were over, and Daley's men had been re-elected and were comfortably seated in their stuffed chairs within their offices, Daley opened the public hearings on hunger. In doing so, however, he pulled a typical Daley ploy.

The hearings were scheduled to begin at nine o'clock in the morning. At exactly that hour, Mayor Daley called the press which had gathered to cover the hearings into his upstairs office for a "special" press conference. The press went, and Daley kept them enthralled with stories and anecdotes until nearly twelve o'clock. What had been advertised as a showdown, a media event, was castrated by Daley's maneuver. When the press people returned to the hearing room, they listened as one of Daley's men read from an official declaration announcing the fact that the council and the mayor's office felt that a commitment of $35 million was out of the question, a burden which the city of Chicago could not accept.

Jesse Jackson obviously felt a little miffed. He had run into Richard Daley in the mayor's territory and had discovered what many of those before him had already known: never play ball in Daley's stadium. All the circumventing which Jackson had done, all the media displays which he had concocted, and all the impassioned pleas which he had made had gone for nothing. His campaign had been emasculated by one Daley maneuver.

On the second day of the hearing, Jackson was angered. He spoke to the council, telling them: "There's not only a generation gap in the City Council, there is a moral gap. While you fiddle, Rome burns!"

Once Jackson had spoken, the City Council dropped

the issue. But later, Mayor Daley would declare hunger to be an emergency, thus paving the way for state and federal funds to be brought into the city to feed the hungry. The move was only a token one, however, and did not result in enough money or food to feed the hungry.

Even though the Chicago political machine had basically defeated Jackson, the country as a whole felt that the young, dynamic leader had made headway in what was a national concern. In Washington, D.C., members of Congress, watching Jackson in Chicago, took up the call. They went on hunger strikes themselves, eating for weeks on a welfare budget and reporting to the Hill on what it was like to be hungry. Congress then passed a bill allocating money to deal with the problem of malnutrition across the nation. President Nixon signed it into law. Later, however, the funds were impounded and the nation's hungry still suffered.

The first round of Jackson's big match with Chicago's political machine had ended. Jackson had been defeated, but in defeat, he had managed to use the media to exploit a horrendous situation and bring to the attention of the country the vision of little children dying of starvation.

It had always been Jackson's genius to promote, to deal with situations which were unpopular and turn them into media events, exposing them to the nation and garnering support which had not existed previously. There are those who continually criticize Jackson for his seeming inability to carry his crusades through on a meaningful level. The fact that Jackson was not able to get Chicago's hungry people fed rings of defeat; but what is important is that Jackson tried, and in trying, he was able to raise the nation's awareness of the problem. A certain amount of understanding must also be accorded Jackson because of the simple fact that he was playing with Daley's baseball in Daley's home park. No one had ever come away from that contest a winner. No one could be that critical of Jackson's defeat.

The taste of politics in Chicago had driven Jackson after the hunger campaign into the arena. He told his people that from that point on, his main center of focus would be on the political machine. Jackson felt that his economic program of bringing money into the black community would continue with much of its energy coming from its own center. He knew that to create radical, permanent changes within Chicago, he would have to strike at the heart of the machine. Success for the poor—both black and white—would come only through a combination of political and economic strength.

As the city elections for 1971 approached, involving the mayoralty race and many positions within the city council, Jesse Jackson organized an arm of Operation Breadbasket designed to instruct and educate the poor blacks of Chicago on the subtleties of the political process. Many of the voters knew what their elected representatives were supposed to do. For many others, the only knowledge they had of their elected officials was the fact that on election day they would bring them something to eat. Insofar as what went on in city chambers, they were totally ignorant. They did not realize that an elected official was supposed to vote in the interest of his or her community, that he or she was responsible to the electorate which had voted them into office.

Jackson was determined to change that, to educate the blacks and transform them into voters who would know why they were voting for a certain candidate.

At the same time, Jackson announced that he was running for mayor of Chicago against Richard Daley. Later, reporters and historians would laugh aloud at the preposterous audacity of Jackson's candidacy. More will be said about this later.

What Jackson intended to do with his new program to educate the electorate was to get black aldermen into office. He wanted not just the color, but the commitment. Already there were blacks serving on Daley's City Council, but all of them were referred to as "houseboys," token representatives of the blacks in that city. They were a silent group, used by Daley whenever the need arose to declare himself a friend of the black man by appearing in public with a black. As a voting bloc and allies of the movement, they were useless. Jackson wanted to move committed people into their office. He also wanted to elect independent liberals, people who were not aligned with the Daley machine.

The goal of electing the independents into office was realized in the election of Fred Hubbard to the post of alderman. The results were tragic, and forever tainted Jackson's effectiveness within the political arena.

Hubbard was an avowed independent, and was running in a district which had long been a stronghold for the Democratic machine of Daley. Jackson sent his troops into the district, educated the voters and pushed hard to get Hubbard elected. On election eve, the results came pouring in. Hubbard, with Jackson's support, had managed to beat the Daley man. Jubilation rang through the movement. They had succeeded in placing a man in office who would listen to the real cries; listen and act without the constraining ropes of the machine holding him forever in a state of limbo. On election night, the victory of Fred Hubbard looked for all of Chicago to be an omen of things to come. The change was in the air, and the initial gate to everlasting victory had been opened.

Fred Hubbard, in a word, was bought. Daley quickly assigned him to head up a federally financed work program, handling the funds that were geared to educate workers, help with the poverty program and even feed some of the hungry. The blacks were delighted. Their man was handling the money, and that meant that it would flow directly into the ghetto.

Someone, however, knew something about Fred Hubbard that neither Jackson nor anyone else had been able to discover. Apparently, Hubbard was a compulsive gambler. Either that or Daley suggested that it would be wise if Hubbard took a little "high rolling" vacation to the West and visit the crap tables of Las Vegas and Reno. Hubbard, slipping thousands of dollars, which had been appropriated to the poor, went on a long jaunt into the gambling dens of America. When he returned, over $100,000 of the people's money lay somewhere between Vegas and Reno—loose change in the pockets of casino owners.

The people of Chicago cried. They had felt hope, had seen the light and it had gone out as quickly as a blackjack from the dealer. No one knew if Hubbard had succumbed to his own weakness, or if Richard Daley had been behind the scheme. It really didn't matter, because once again, all the thunder had been stolen.

The election that year wasn't a total loss, however. Jackson managed to help two councilmen, both blacks, who managed to penetrate the machine and oust Daley candidates. But the victory was small compared to the losses.

The 1971 elections provided a scenario for Daley that would result in him temporarily losing face as a political animal. Jackson entered the race for mayor for a number of reasons, all being buried beneath the publicity of the fiasco that was to come. Initially, Jackson sought to open the doors for independents to get on Chicago's ballots without going through the process of getting signatures and dealing with Daley's certification control. Also, he was seeking to establish a voting bloc of Chicago's half million independent voters through a third party which he called the Bread 'n Butter party. Basically, Jackson was trying to destroy the age-old tradition of voting the slate in Chicago. This meant that when a voter voted for his local alderman, he would also vote straight down the line for the other Democratic candidates listed. So, one man giving a voter a chicken would provide the votes for his fellow Daley Democrats and for Daley himself. Jackson was attempting to get Chicago blacks to learn how to crossover, to vote back and forth between the Republican and the Democratic candidates. He felt that by putting himself on the ballot, he would at least motivate his thousands of followers to move their pencils into another column.

Jackson took his petitions to get on the ballot through the courts, all the way to the Supreme Court. However,

111

the system in Chicago which had been set up through Daley's connections with the state judicial organization resulted in defeat. Jackson could not overcome the road-block which existed for an independent to get his name on the ballet. He was testing it, seeing if the legal voices presiding from the bench were ready to turn things around. As it happened, they were not.

During his court battles, Jesse Jackson wavered back and forth between his commitments to run for mayor. Ralph Abernathy even supported him as a fine alternative between the Republicans and the Democrats. But Jackson, always playing for the media, moved back and forth. People began to take him less seriously. Jackson lost some credibility during those months in early 1971 because many white liberals and many blacks had come out in support of him. Theirs was an earnest endorsement. Jackson's wavering, his almost off-handed treatment of his own intentions confused his supporters. Many would feel that Jackson was using them for his own publicity stunts.

Unfortunately, the chaos and confusion during the 1971 elections disrupted what could have been the beginnings of a separate, and powerful new machine within Chicago. With Jackson's electoral education plan, his move to organize precincts and people for this particular election, and the few dents that were actually made into Daley's machine, a beginning was emerging. It was a slow beginning but one which, nurtured and molded, could have resulted in a voter bloc that was educated and in touch with one another. After the 1971 elections, and the scandals that followed, whatever organization had been built disintegrated. Although the swing would continue in slow motion away from Daley, Daley himself would still wield all the power. In 1971, Daley was elected to his fifth term, and things were still under his thumb. Even his concern over Jackson's candidacy had faded after the court decision which prevented Jackson from placing his name on the ballot.

As 1972 approached, Richard Daley felt that his kingdom, although shifting slightly, was still his. The presidential primaries were approaching with the Democratic convention itself in Miami. Daley was looking forward to his usual role as kingmaker within the Democratic party.

That was before a relatively unknown senator from South Dakota named George McGovern began making his move; and it was before Jesse Jackson leaped into the infamous credentials battle prior to the Miami convention that would result in the impossible—the unseating of King Daley from his throne of power on the floor of the convention. The battle was approaching, and Jackson would be there, sword waving and glinting beneath the Florida sun.

As 1972 approached, America was moving into a new era of politics. The system had showed signs of change throughout the previous five years, but the greatest change of all was the registration of huge numbers of blacks to vote. This occurred after the Voter Rights Bill of 1965, and as a result of Martin Luther King's voter registration drives through the South. In the early sixties, the black man simply did not vote; in 1972, there were enough blacks voting to change the political color in America. Blacks had been voted into offices throughout the country—as mayors, congressmen, state legislators and assemblymen. The black voting bloc was beginning to show its muscle, and that muscle would have to be taken into consideration by any candidate running for national office.

As the primaries and National Conventions approached in 1972, the black spokesmen throughout the country were talking about the new power which they possessed. They spoke about delegates to the conventions being ''real'' blacks, and not appointees chosen by the white power-brokers to ostensibly represent an entire race of people. Julian Bond and others spoke in terms of exerting real thrust within the party, showing muscle in the selection of candidates from the president on down.

The establishment was looking at the rise of blacks within the political community with a certain amount of reservation. Yet most of the spokesmen who did carry political clout were not radicals or violent revolutionaries. They were men who worked within the system, and they were men who could be dealt with. The white power-brokers understood that in the Democratic party, the swing would be toward human rights, a swing that was long over-due. Hubert Humphrey's nomination beneath Richard Daley's police thugs in 1968, they hoped, had washed clean the image of the Democratic party as one that was liberal in voice, but right wing in action. They were looking towards the 1972 election as the beginning of a new coalition between the liberals, and anti-war elements, the minorities and the poor. The Democratic party would once again be the party of the people.

Jesse Jackson was at the time sitting outside the political spectrum. He was not a Democrat, nor was he a

Republican. He had supported men of both persuasions, and had thus labeled himself a political independent. So, early in 1971 when Jackson announced the formation of a third political party, the Liberation Party, people held their breath. They were truly shocked when Jackson added that the purpose of his new party would be to elect a black to the presidency of the United States; or to use its position to force the Democrats in 1972 to run a black as vice-president.

The press reacted to Jackson's announcement as though the man had flipped on over to the other side of sanity. The black movement was just beginning to make headway within the established political spectrum, and it seemed outrageous that Jackson would make such a gigantic leap into no man's land.

The reaction to the idea of a third party throughout the political scene was basically negative. Most black leaders felt that to organize the nation's blacks on such a scale would be next to impossible. They felt that blacks did not identify themselves with the power of the vote, and the politics still remained somewhat meaningless as an avenue towards improvement. To ask people, especially incumbent politicians, to jump their allegiance with a certain party, they suggested, would be next to impossible.

Jackson persisted with his notion, and event went so far as to name Congressman John Conyers to head up the ticket of the Liberation Party. The Black Caucus in Congress, composed of the black representatives from around the country, were angry with Jackson for naming Conyers. They felt that Jackson was destroying unity, and once again the charge of stealing headlines was leveled at

Jackson.

Then practically out of nowhere, came Congresswoman Shirley Chisholm to announce that she, too, was running for the presidency. Now, Jackson lost his uniqueness. Besides throwing in her hat as a black, Chisholm was throwing it in as a woman. The press loved her. She was outspoken, caustic and determined as she spoke in a powerful voice that seemed too large for her petite frame. But Shirley Chisholm was on shaky ground with blacks, even with those men who were disgruntled with Jesse Jackson and his ploys. The reason for this is an interesting one.

Shirley Chisholm had come through the ranks not so much as a black, but as a woman. It was a time of the emerging feminist movement, and Shirley was considered to be one of the more outspoken feminists in the nation. The white press liked her—she was spunky and hard-headed, and possessed a wry sense of humor. The biggest problem with Chisholm, however, was that she was not liked by black men.

Psychologically, it is easy to see why this state of affairs existed. The black man was just beginning to find his own sense of manhood in a country which had once called him only three-eighths of a man. Through struggle, sacrifice and bloodshed, the black man was beginning to emerge as a full citizen. During the years of struggle, it was the man who suffered incredible blows to his ego. The woman suffered just as much, but her sense of identity was more ensconced within the home, raising children and keeping her man happy. He was expected to go out into the world, a white world, to make his living and bring a decent life home to his family. He had suffered for his inability to do that. He had not been called a man, and he had fought back to regain that manhood.

Shirley Chisholm, basically, had leaped years ahead of her time in assuming the role of a woman's liberationist. She worked hand-in-hand with the Gloria Steinems and Bella Abzugs in proclaiming rights for females. The blacks watched her standing there with two white women, upper middle class women who had lived in white America and had everything white America has to offer. It was kind of like watching a black protesting along with whites the banning of rollerskating on a white beach when, at home, that black's family was trying to avoid rats and trying to feed itself.

The tension between Chisholm and the black leadership was high, and served to split the unity between them.

In April of 1971, the black powerbrokers from across the country gathered in Gary, Indiana for the Black National Convention. The purpose of the convention was to unite the black voting bloc into one singular thrust, to once and for all bring all the elements of the movement together in order to achieve power at the polls.

However, the Black Convention dissolved into a ragtag of disunity. The blacks were showing themselves to be just as diverse and separatist as the white man.

Shirley Chisholm did not appear at the convention, although the feelings towards her had swung and there was talk of nominating her as a candidate. Jesse Jackson was there, and called for the rise of a third party. People booed. Black leaders spoke, but there was not a uniform sense of purpose. There was no direction, and Jesse Jackson found himself unable to wield power or to formulate an opinion.

At the convention, most of the delegates were already behind George McGovern. The strategy of forcing the black community into one powerful fist which could be used as a power lever against the Democrats during the upcoming convention had failed miserably. The black delegates had gone to the power that be, that is, to McGovern and what they felt was a reasonable machine, one which would produce victory in the upcoming elections.

The politics of the previous year, then, had resulted in a state of chaos among the black leadership. From the Black Convention had come three proposals, all separate and developed from individual sources. The Jackson Economic Bill of Rights, the Black Agenda and the Black Bill of Rights. A candidate who desired the support of the black voters and delegates would have to endorse one of the three. George McGovern privately endorsed all three but made no mention of any one of them at the Convention.

Thus, the bold move toward real black power through a voting coalition that had the power to sway the election failed. Jackson's Liberation Party seemed to dissolve without even a murmur, and the Black National Convention drowned in its own sea of disharmony. As the Democratic Convention approached, the only big difference between this year and years past was the fact that delegates were drawn from a wider cross section of the American public.

The primary season during the spring of 1972 had laid the foundation for the bizarre political circus that would emerge in Miami later that summer. Richard Nixon, on the

Republican side, was hiding out in the White House, sweeping primaries and expected a shoo-in as an incumbent nominee. Murmurs about the break-in at the Watergate Hotel were just rising to the surface.

On the Democratic side, Ed Muskie was breaking down on the campaign trail, having been abused and assaulted by a campaign of dirty tricks that would be exposed years later as the true machinations of the Nixonian empire came to light. George McGovern, riding a crest built upon the support of the anti-war movement and the liberal factions was sweeping into the nomination.

They came to Miami that summer, thousands of people never before seen at a national convention. Minorities were prevalent, as were young people, hippies, yippies and housewives. They were a cross section of America 1972, all claiming delegate seats on the convention floor. Battles raged as separate delegations attempted to get themselves seated. As an orderly process of an orderly political machine, the Democratic National Convention was a complete and utter fiasco. But as a challenge to the old guard, as a thrust against the powerbrokers who defended Mayor Richard Daley as he threw his Chicago police brutality against demonstrators at the Convention in 1968, the convention was effective. The mood in Miami was different, and the kingpins of the party were nervous. It appeared as though the people had finally come to a convention, come to stake their claim in the American political process.

Mayor Daley looked forward to Miami with his usual powerbroker smile and entourage of lackeys and yes men. Ever since anyone could remember, Richard Daley had sat in the Chicago delegation, a phone by his side; power emanating from his chair. Chicago and Cook County, thus Illinois, had always been a powerful lever in the election for president. It was assumed that to win at the Democratic National Convention, you had to have Richard Daley at your side. Daley had no reason to believe that things would be any different this year in Miami. He was all set with his delegation of fifty-nine delegates and thirty-one alternates. All were supposedly uncommitted and free to vote in any manner they chose, but everyone on the floor would know that each member of the Chicago delegation had been instructed by Daley as to how they would cast their vote. Daley was the only vote that really counted, and whichever way he went, so went the delegation.

As they arrived in Chicago, Daley and his people did not think about 1968 and Senator George McGovern and the incredibly far-reaching reform which McGovern had pushed through that convention. During that disastrous convention, George McGovern had gotten a complete revision of delegate selection process passed. The effects of McGovern's reform would not be felt until 1972. It would hit Mayor Daley directly in the gut of his political power.

The delegate reform which McGovern had pushed for stated that all delegations were to be chosen on an open basis, and that delegates were to be representative of the people of the electoral district. They were also to be representative of the various minorities and sexes, a percentage equal to that of the percentage of the population as a whole.

Mayor Daley ignored the new rules, and balked when reporters suggested that he may be in violation of them. Daley would bring his delegation to the convention as he always had, hand-picking those men who remained loyal to him, picking as many blacks as he damned well pleased, and powerbroking his delegation exactly as he had done in the past.

Jesse Jackson watched Daley's hand-picked delegation and licked his chops. He now had a vehicle with which to attack the man who had so often stumped himself and his hero, Martin Luther King. Together with a white alderman from Chicago, William Singer, Jackson challenged the right of Daley's delegation to be seated on the convention floor.

The hearings which would decide the legality of Daley's delegation were held in Chicago only a month prior to the convention. The hearings began on a bad note for Jesse Jackson when the hearing officer assigned to the case by the credentials chairman of the Democratic party, Mrs. Patricia Harris, suddenly resigned after being pressured to do so by one of Daley's aldermen. Mrs. Harris responded quickly by sending a black attorney by the name of Cecil Poole into Chicago to conduct the hearings.

Richard Daley and his boys were just a little perturbed over this new hearing officer. They approached Poole with their usual implied threats, and tried to use the solid power of the machine to convince Poole that he should get the hearings over with as quickly as possible and send Jesse Jackson back into the Southside to preach to his black followers instead of messing around with delegations to the national convention.

Cecil Poole was not a Tom. He was a hard-nosed lawyer who did not play favorites. When Jackson appeared before his committee, Poole made Jackson look ridiculous as he cross-examined him with a sharp tongue and a quick mind. Ironically, it was revealed during Jackson's testimony that Jesse had never bothered to vote. This caused an uproar among his critics, but did not affect the outcome of the hearings themselves.

Daley's boys were also cross-examined by Poole, and they didn't fare much better. Poole was not about to compromise his position and allow the Chicago machine to steamroll him. He was ready for Daley, and he remained strong during the hearings. The outcome was that Poole and the hearing committee decided that Daley had, indeed, violated the rules for selection of delegates to the national convention, and the Democratic party called for an open election in Chicago in order to select a new delegation.

Eight locations were then selected where the people of Chicago could vote for their delegates. On the day of the elections, Daley let loose his hoodlums and showed Chicago what being heir to Al Capone was really all about. Hundreds of Daley men strolled election meetings, pushing organizers, hitting people, pushing men to the floor. Intimidation was the name of the game, and Daley was pulling out all the stops.

Some of the election meetings were rescheduled. At the largest one held at a Sheraton Hotel, Jesse Jackson arrived prepared for Richard Daley's army. Surrounding him were approximately one hundred of Chicago's toughest blacks. The mean, ominous looking cats surrounded Jackson and confronted Daley's men. They moved stealthily, and soon, Daley's men realized that they had been outthugged by Jackson.

The election of the new slate of delegates to the convention had barely missed turning into an all-out war between the armies of Daley and the armies of Jackson. But finally, the slate was elected. Daley's power hold on the Democratic Convention had disappeared.

For the liberals in the nation, and the people in the movement, Jesse Jackson was a hero. He had finally managed to do what no other man had ever been able—to beat the King of Chicago. Jackson had always wanted to push himself into the position of powerbroker, to use that position to force candidates and officials into endorsing and promoting his programs. Now it appeared that he had the chance.

After the new slate had been elected, Richard Daley sat back and fumed. He was not inactive. He took away Jesse Jackson's personal police protection. Shortly afterwards, Jesse's office was firebombed. Jackson began to receive threats on his and his family's life. The backlash forced Jackson to move his wife and children out of Chicago, at least until the heat died down. Threats from the mayor were not much fun, and everyone in the country knew just how deep Lake Michigan was, and how a man could disappear forever into its dark depths.

Jesse Jackson paid a high price for his victory over Richard Daley. Instead of savoring the fruits of that victory, Jackson immediately turned around and did the unthinkable—he offered Daley a compromise on the delegation seating, suggesting that his delegation split the chairs with Daley's delegation.

The movement people and the liberals were horrified by Jackson's compromise offering. This move on Jackson's part was only indicative of his instinct for survival. Jackson knew very well that Chicago, where he worked and lived, and the Democratic Convention would not ever be without Daley, even if the mayor was not seated on the convention floor. More than one president had credited Daley with getting him elected into office. Beyond Jackson and his delegation victory lay the rest of the country. Whoever was nominated would somehow have to make up with Daley, and Jackson knew that if that arrangement involved a sacrifice, then Jackson would be the one to go.

Compromise with Richard Daley, although a disappointment to many, was a wise and worldly position for Jackson to take. The machine was somewhat on the decline, yet Daley still wielded incredible power. Jackson, as well as his fellow Democrats, would have to work with Daley in the future. Jackson had finally arrived at a position of power where he could bargain on an equal level with Daley. Offering Daley the compromise was a means of Jackson saying: "Okay, we're now both playing in the big leagues, so let's play like pros."

Richard Daley, however, was not about to make deals with a black man especially from a position of weakness. He refused to compromise, and for the first time since anyone could remember, Richard Daley sat out the Democratic Convention at home.

Jesse Jackson did attend the convention, and was hailed as a hero by many of the delegates. He addressed the convention and turned the place upside down with his rhetoric. Jackson had truly arrived on the national scene as a result of defeating his old nemesis, Richard Daley.

The remainder of the convention allowed Jesse Jackson to play the role of powerbroker to a certain extent. Even as the nomination for George McGovern was gaining impetus, Shirley Chisholm was also making a run. The black hierarchy at the convention desperately wanted to release delegates so that they could vote for Chisholm. Jackson, having been promised support of his programs by McGovern, went onto the convention floor and successfully manipulated delegates to stay with McGovern. He was personally responsible for stopping the Chisholm tide. Political experts contend that this was the wisest, most realistic approach. They say, even after McGovern's terrible defeat in the November elections, that the situation would have been much worse had Chisholm brought about a compromise candidate.

At the time of his nomination, George McGovern represented the most realistic hopes for blacks, the anti-war people and the minorities throughout the country. That hope, however, would fade quickly.

Even before the convention sounded the adjourning gavel, the black power structure felt betrayed by George McGovern. They had gathered together to select a name to present to the nominee for consideration as his running mate in November. Surprisingly, and without their consultation, McGovern announced that Thomas Eagleton would be his choice for vice-president.

Jackson and his fellow blacks were angered by the decision, angered because they had no choice in the matter. Disappointment went even further when, during his acceptance speech, McGovern failed to endorse the programs which he privately endorsed only weeks before.

Yet, even with their disappointment with McGovern, the

blacks felt they had to align themselves with him. After all, the man to defeat in 1972 was Richard Nixon, a long avowed enemy of the Civil Rights Movement, a man who had openly stated that changes in human rights would have to take many more years than the blacks were willing to give it. So support from the black community was given to McGovern.

Support, however, was not what McGovern needed. What George really needed was a campaign manager and staff with some amount of political shrewdness. It was becoming evident that George McGovern was a decent, honest guy but he seemed to lack the calculating, manipulative character necessary in politics. His choice of Eagleton was a true indicator that trouble lay ahead.

The press, the Republicans and most of the country jumped all over McGovern when it was learned that the man who might be a heartbeat away from the most powerful office in the world had undergone treatment for mental disorders in his home state of Missouri. The Eagleton affair cracked the thin coating of McGovern's credibility for all time. George wavered from support to non-support, and finally accepted Eagleton's resignation of his nomination.

Jesse Jackson, who had committed himself to McGovern, saw the writing on the wall with the Eagleton affair. He quickly faded into the background, neither supporting nor condemning McGovern's actions. Jackson had seen McGovern turn enough times in the winds of politics to know that the best position might be no position at all. Jackson wanted a good man in office, a man who would stay honest and supportive of the black man in America.

Jackson was shrewd enough to understand that to attach one's lifeboat to a sinking ship, no matter how nice or thoughtful that ship might be, was a move which could result in his own drowning.

Besides, McGovern had chosen Eagleton without asking the blacks at the convention what they thought. That was a political blunder of the highest order. Even if the decision is firmly locked in, it is considered a traditional show of good political sense to flatter those who have helped you to get nominated by listening to their suggestions and involving them in the decision making process. McGovern turned his back on this tradition, and I think, paid for it when the Eagleton affair exploded.

McGovern had also failed to mention the proposals which had been drawn up at the Black Convention, and that must have hurt. Jesse Jackson must have felt some resentment towards McGovern at this time. After all, Jackson had tried to compromise with Daley, bringing down the wrath of the black press and liberal establishment in order to sew the crack in the Democratic power structure. That gesture had been made in an effort to provide McGovern with the backing he would need to get elected. Jackson had roamed the floor of the Convention, stopping a movement for Shirley Chisholm which, had it succeeded, most certainly would have resulted in a compromise candidate other than McGovern.

So, when the ship began to sink, Jesse Jackson did not feel obligated to remain on board. He jumped quickly. When you consider the mismanagement and mistakes of the McGovern candidacy, it appears that Jesse Jackson was using his brains at a time when everyone else seemed to have left them at home.

Jesse Jackson had played his political games and had changed the face of the Democratic party. Since 1969, he had been responsible for dramatic changes within Chicago. He had been chaotic, and not always consistent in his movements, but he had opened the door. The Daley machine had been permanently weakened, and Jackson had been responsible. The look of Chicago voters had changed. Jesse Jackson had begun to learn how to deal with Richard Daley.

Jesse Jackson and Richard Daley were still avowed enemies, but both men had gained a new respect for the other. Both enjoyed power and understood it. Both had succeeded in developing a machine that could be used to gain their ends. Jesse Jackson was now playing in another league, and Richard Daley knew that would make a difference. It would allow the two men to huddle privately in Daley's suite and possibly speak on equal terms with one another. Some people said that Jesse Jackson, beginning with his compromise proposal to Daley on the delegation question, was selling out. But those who understood the netherworld of politics where there is neither black nor white felt that Jesse Jackson had finally learned how to deal with the powers that be.

Jackson founded Push For Excellence in the early 1970s to encourage education among young blacks and to discourage the use of drugs among America's teens.

Jesse Jackson's Rainbow Coalition (as symbolized by the sign at the bottom of this photograph) was designed to bring people of all colors together in the common cause of electing Jackson to the White House.

Chapter 6

Push For Excellence

By the time Richard Nixon took the oath of office on the steps of the Capitol in 1973, Jesse Jackson was a national figure. He was the main spokesman for the black movement, the man to whom the press turned for answers whenever a question of black attitude arose. Jesse Jackson had become famous both for his dealings with Richard Daley and for the financial success of Operation Breadbasket.

Yet, there were critics. People who said that Jesse Jackson was nothing more than an astute, clever, black capitalist who was using the struggle for freedom of the nation's twenty-five million blacks as a means of putting money into the pockets of business associates, as well as into his own pocket. The facts backed these critics' charges. Jackson was becoming a wealthy man and so were his business friends. Jackson was moving in circles reserved for the beautiful people. He had as his friends movie stars, entertainers and famous athletes. With his power base in Chicago, his gorgeous home and his financial power, Jesse Jackson appeared to have it made. The people who felt that a national civil rights leader should act like a martyr were disgruntled.

The critics were far outnumbered by his fans. Jesse Jackson had become a hero to many. His Saturday morning rallies with Operation Breadbasket were drawing well, and were being carried over a network of radio stations spanning the country. People gathered wherever the dynamic speaker appeared. His message had become less political now, and Jackson concentrated once more on black capitalism, on the power which blacks would have if they made their own communities economically strong.

Touring the country, Jackson delivered his message of black pride to millions of people—in auditoriums, stadiums and schools. His cry of ''I am somebody'' was chanted by adoring fans, people who felt a tingle of excitement and not a little amount of hope as the Baptist preacher thrilled them with his voice and his words. Jackson would appear on stage wearing a buckskin jacket and tight Levis, his hair billowing in a styled Afro, and he would enchant his audiences. He had risen to the top, he was the hippest of the hip. He was a black cat that had made it. He lived well, ate well and seemed to be having a lot of fun.

In the eyes of his younger audiences, Jesse Jackson was

a folk hero. He was a sensuous man, and they related to that. He was masculine, powerful and audacious. He was different from Dr. King in that he was flashy. Dudes driving long, lean Cadillacs could relate to him. Young students wearing superfly hats and charming ladies could relate to him. Housewives living in Watts fantasized about him. And businessmen dealing in the expanding world of black commerce respected and dealt with him.

Jesse Jackson, by 1975, was flying high with an adoring public behind him. But then, as a result of his tours which led him into city schools throughout the country, he began talking about the young people in a way which many thought at the time "unhip." Jackson had been a kind of superfly-straight hero to many young blacks, and suddenly he began telling these kids that they were going the wrong way worshipping the image of the black man as superdude. As Jackson turned his attention to the young generation, he began to see an entire group of kids coming into adulthood unprepared and without the necessary tools to make the changes that would be necessary in the future.

As he toured the nation's schools, Jesse Jackson saw the crime, the dress codes of the black youngsters, the marijuana and dope, the affected attitudes and the general lack of effort among the thousands of black students whom he addressed. He saw that while the adults had been fighting on the lines, trying to push for change, the children were being left behind to deal with a culture that Jackson felt was depraved. As Jackson put it: "Our schools are infested with a steady diet of vandalism, violence, drugs, intercourse without discourse, alcohol and television addiction. The result," added Jackson, "was a generation bred to be passive and superficial."

What Jackson saw among the young was the same thing many white people had been noticing with their own offspring. It was a malady that was sweeping across America. Four to five hours a night in front of the television set, watching inane shows and ridiculous comedies, the influx of drugs into the school system where teenagers were spending more time to score Quaaludes than they were studying; a preoccupation with sex in dress codes and distracting behavior; and a total neglect of education in the traditional sense. The students coming out of the nation's schools were often illiterate, and still they were admitted to colleges where they were given inconsequential degrees. The generation, as Jackson saw it, was being molded by a flashy, glitter-craving society. Plastic fantastic had become the foundation of an entire generation. Jesse Jackson decided that he would try to do something to stop it, at least among the black children who had so much further to go than the white children.

What began as a reaction against the morality of America soon turned into a program. Jackson called his brainchild PUSH FOR EXCELLENCE, or in the shorter version, PUSH-Excel.

The essential ingredients of PUSH-Excel were based on a foundation of traditional values. Jackson saw the problem of the young generation as one in which they were floundering in a world without parental leadership and without the traditional sense of discipline which emanates from the parents. "Only by re-establishing moral authority," Jackson stated, "that is, our believability, our trustworthiness, our caring—can we demand discipline and have it perceived as therapy and not punishment.''

Jackson's program for PUSH-Excel was based on a program of disciplines designed to get the young black student back into the mainstream of education; a program that was also designed to promote black students to excel. In order to achieve the goal of educating and preparing students for the future, Jackson also insisted that the parents become involved with their children's education. Using a four point program, Jackson suggested that the parents meet their children's teachers and exchange phone numbers; that they pick up their children's test scores; and that parents turn off the television set and radio for at least two hours every night.

As Jackson toured the country, establishing PUSH-Excel programs in school districts in major cities, the reaction to his program from parents and teachers has been good. Jackson has provided parents with a means of affecting their child's growth. Helplessness within the black community with regard to the raising of offspring has always been a problem. Parents, struggling to the point of exhaustion merely to keep their survival effort afloat, have often not had the energy to deal with their own children. When they did find that energy, it was tough to get through.

The black children of America have been through a traumatic number of changes. They have instinctively felt one step away below the white children. So, when the political system shifts or moves through a tragedy such as the assassination of a Kennedy or a King, the children find it difficult to relate. The problem exhibited itself with adults who felt so disenfranchised with the system that they failed to register to vote during King's voter registration drive in Chicago.

Feeling themselves far away from the mainstream, and unable to participate, the black youth turned toward role models. These models were presented to them via movies and television. Superflys and others of the inner city, wearing fine threads and driving long, sleek Cadillacs, were presented to the kids as heroes. Many young men dressed and acted like the characters they saw in films, ignoring their own identities.

Music has also played a huge role in defining the culture of the black youth. Soul music, black disco and jazz have become readily identifiable with black youth, and many young blacks relate to music more readily than to their own futures.

What Jackson has been trying to tell the young is that the culture as it now stands is programming them into a subservient lifestyle. Kids growing up watching television and listening to music will be prepared for little more than sweeping floors or working on an assembly line. Jackson sees the culture as evil, one that has been designed and promoted by the white man to keep the generation in a complete state of ignorance. What Jackson says could be true as well for the white culture and what is happening to its youth.

Jackson until recently concentrated more on his own people, preaching across the country for the need to educate, the need for students to move out of the electronic culture and begin to use their minds.

It is hard to imagine any other man but Jesse Jackson

being able to get away with this kind of talk. It is difficult to think of a Ralph Abernathy standing up in front of a group of black students wearing sharp clothes, and a smirk, and telling them to stop worrying about their movie images. Jesse Jackson has been able to do all this. He is hip enough himself, sharp enough and successful enough on a level that counts. Jackson's run-ins with those kids he is trying to convert give evidence to his ability to relate to them.

Jackson has the image and the reputation to be able to redefine black manhood. He will stand in front of a group of high school students and say: "Brothers, you're not a man because you can kill somebody. You're not a man because you can make a baby. They can make babies through artificial insemination. Imbeciles can make babies. Fools can make babies. You're a man only if you can raise a baby, protect a baby and provide for a baby." Jesse Jackson can say that to a crowd of young men who have watched the violence, watched the heroes strutting their stuff, and make it stick. They listen to Jesse Jackson because Jackson is a new kind of hero.

After a speech one evening several years ago, a young man approached Jesse Jackson and began talking. The young man was wearing a wide brimmed superfly hat, and was objecting to the fact that Jackson had demanded that every hat be removed while he was speaking. The young man told Jackson that it didn't make any difference what lay on the head, that the real meaning lay inside the head. Jackson listened and nodded, then spoke about the real world. He told the young man that if he went in for a job interview wearing the hat, no one would bother long enough with him to find out what lay inside his skull. The young man nodded, removed his hat and understood. Jackson speaks sense with these youngsters because he can talk the language of money.

It was during his speech about being a man, that Jackson addressed the ladies in the crowd. They had laughed and giggled when Jackson had told the audience that "an imbecile can make a baby." He turned to the women and said, "There's another side to it, sisters. If you are to deserve the kind of man you cheer for, you cannot spend more time in school on the cultivation of your bosom than your books. If you are to be the right kind of woman, you cannot have a fully developed bottom and a half developed brain. A donkey got an ass, but he ain't got no sense." The audience loved it. They laughed, and they understood. And they remembered.

It is this mixture of hipness, and tradition, old fashioned common sense that works so effectively for Jackson when he speaks to students. He does not talk in the abstract about rewards after death, he does not speak in political terms. He just talks common sense, and he talks about a lifestyle and position in the world that everyone wants.

With his campaign for excellence, Jesse Jackson also began to hit stereotypes that have existed in America for many decades—that of the black man as an athlete. There are thousands of kids in ghetto playgrounds throughout America playing baseball, dreaming of being Reggie Jackson; thousands more throwing a basketball through a hoop and having visions of Dr. J.; and thousands more running an end sweep seeing themselves as O.J. Simpson. For the young black in America, athletics on a professional level has long held the greatest hope for success, wealth and fame. Jesse Jackson will stand in front of an all-black high school football team and remind them that isn't necessarily so.

Many black athletes are joining Jackson in his campaign to steer black youth into academics and out of athletics. These are men who themselves have achieved the dream. But they will stand with Jackson and begin quoting statistics. How many young black basketball players, being the star of their neighborhoods, then their high schools, and maybe their colleges, will ever make it to the pros? How about baseball? There are less than three hundred major baseball league players in America. There are nearly 200 million people. And they go on, telling these children that there are other role models to look up to, men who have made it with their brains and not their biceps. Jesse Jackson, standing before them, successful and famous, is the first example that will be thrust at the kids.

Politically, Jackson's PUSH-Excel program is an interesting one when you take into consideration the history of the black movement over the last twenty years. During the sixties, the movement was divided into a number of philosophies. There was Martin Luther King's program of change within and through the system through nonviolence. There was the Black Panther Party and its revolutionary dictates of change through violence. And there were the Black Muslims, headed by Malcolm X, who called for a state of hatred to exist between blacks and whites, one which he hoped would result in an eventual separate state for black men and women. In the early seventies, Jesse Jackson began calling for a change within the system through economic strength. Jackson was sending his mesage out to his people that black capitalism was the way to go—get money into the ghettos and into the pockets of black businessmen. Blacks would then have the wherewithal and the political clout to begin demanding changes within the system.

All of these programs had one thing in common—they were all directed toward an exterior change. Once the blacks were massed together, the programs called for them to move as one against injustice. The techniques were different, but they all were directed toward a common enemy.

With PUSH-Excel, Jackson has turned the movement inwards. He has begun telling the kids that progress and change will come only from the perfection of the individual. He has thrust the responsibility of change onto the individual. That burden had formerly rested with various portions and institutions of society. But now, the emphasis, with Jackson's program, is changing.

There are some critics of PUSH-Excel who argue that Jackson has placed the burden too heavily upon the shoulders of the young. They say that there are still evils within society, evils which exist outside the immediate abilities of the young that should be noted, and corrected. They argue that Jackson is playing into the hands of the white man by excusing the ghettos, the inadequate schooling, the injustice and throwing all of the weight onto the kid's attitude toward school.

The argument does have merit. Those who criticize the program, I believe, are missing one vital point. As Jackson and others before him discovered during their bouts with political machines, an uneducated electorate is practically useless in exercising its power to create change. Only the educated voter, aware of other process and how it works, can achieve some result which will benefit himself and his people down the road. As Jackson discovered, it is extremely difficult to educate those people who have been mired throughout their adult lives in the sense-crushing environment of the ghetto. Those people in the Southside of Chicago, who voted for the alderman because on election day or at Christmas they brought them a dinner, were difficult people to educate. Their stomachs were talking, not their brains. It seems that Jackson understood this, and understood that only through the education of the young could a future generation be ready for change through the voting process. Only with an enlightened generation could the movement drop its suicidal pretensions to violence and begin to gain strength through intelligent political and economic means.

It also seems that the critics of Jackson's program are missing another, more subtle point. While Jackson is trying to organize the black teachers, parents and students to redefine their own education system, and create a discipline that works, the American school system is degenerating into an abyss of illiteracy and non-productivity. The statistics which are emerging from the schools are astounding. There is a definite crisis in education, and the whites as well as the blacks are suffering.

By 1984 the crisis within black education had a leader, a man who had the power, the charisma and the energy to make a change. Jesse Jackson speaks not only for education, but for dignity, survival and economic gain. The white system had no one speaking for it, the white children were also drifting further and further into their television sets and drug-induced rock concert stupors.

Operation PUSH-Excel showed some tremendous results in the beginning. For example, in Kansas City's predominantly black Central High School during the 1976-77 school year, nearly 500 students out of a total of 1,300 were absent each day. During the school year of 1978, the average absenteeism was down to 200 students per day. A student pride association had been started, modeling itself after Jesse Jackson's credo, and the result had been a newly formed pride in their school. The students had carpeted the auditorium, planted trees and painted murals on the walls. School had become a place of respect instead of an institution of scorn. Jackson had shown them a purpose in education, a reason to be there, and that seemed to be all the students needed.

In Chicago, the PUSH-Excel program showed some good results, also. At Marshall High School, the Chicago police once roamed the campus trying to keep order and attempting to keep the number of knifings and killing down. By 1978, these same policemen were working as counselors. Within the academic arena, students were reacting directly to Jackson's plea for academic excellence by enrolling in advanced English, math and science classes. At a high school in Los Angeles, the student rate of absenteeism dropped from thirty-five to twelve percent.

When Jackson goes into a ghetto school with his message, the students listen. More importantly, the principals and teachers also listen. In the past Jackson has provided these public servants with a new glimmer of hope, something which has been missing from their profession for a long long time.

A high school teacher in Los Angeles, who worked with the Excel program, told me that, "The program turned the kids around. I could see a difference in their attitudes, the way they dress, and the way they relate to me. Jackson made the teachers an extension of himself, and when a student he has reached sees me, he or she is looking at Jackson."

The involvement of the parents, the teachers and the students in forming a coalition for learning was a successful one in the beginning. Too, when Jackson took his message into the white community, people listened. Jackson called for an agreement between society and his younger black generation. He called for the whites to recognize progress and to assimilate that progress into their own culture. Jackson warned those whites whom he addressed that without basic, civilized responses to education and the new black generation, civilization itself would come to a "dead end."

The establishment responded positively to Jackson's Excel program. The federal government began to untie the purse strings and allow a cash flow into the schools working under the program. The white officials who listened to Jackson, and watched the response his speeches evoked, began to understand the positive thrust of the Excel program could result in positive gains for society as a whole. Once again, Jackson was not pushing people into a political corner where they had to commit themselves to a revolutionary act. Instead, he incorporated those values which white society has long held to be near and dear and demonstrated that the black man respects those same qualities.

Unfortunately, the Excel program eventually fell short of original expectations. Giving Washington High School in Los Angeles as an example, Joseph Nazel has said: "As long as Jackson was on hand, the program worked. At Washington the success rate in signing up students to commit to the program was excellent, the school administration got behind it and clamped on troublemakers or kids involved in drugs and illegal activities. But without Jackson's charisma, the kids gradually lost enthusiasm. I think you'd have to say that, at this point during his second (1988) bid for the presidency, it's really hard to say how successful the program was. Certainly it did some good but I'd expect many of those who embraced it with such enthusiasm in the beginning would probably say they were eventually disappointed."

Gradually, as Jackson entered politics, he turned the operation of PUSH-Excel over to others.

Nevertheless, Jackson is still able to get his message across to young people and especially when he appears before them in person. During several emotionally charged appearances at Los Angeles and San Francisco area schools and colleges during his 1988 campaign, he again called on students to make a commitment to the principles of PUSH-Excel, asking them to stand up, then step forth.

What began as a trickle of young people, most black but including some whites and Latinos, quickly became a flood, many of them with tears streaming down their faces.

Jesse Jackson's mesage to the young is simple; but it is effective and positive. He is at once giving them responsibility and a means of carrying out that responsibility.

To an entire segment of society—that which is involved in education—which has so long been taken for granted and ignored, Jackson has provided hope.

Jesse Jackson understands the basic formulas for success. He knows that nothing will ever change the past three hundred years. He realizes that human nature is a force that exists and must be dealt with. And he knows that when it comes down to it, only the indiviual will ever be able to effect true change. As Jackson said in one of his many speeches: "Nobody will stop us from killing ourselves. Nobody will make us catch up. We have to rely on ourselves to overcome history."

Jesse Jackson on the campaign trail in 1988, backed by leaders of his Rainbow Coalition.

Chapter 7

Jesse and the Media:
Love at First Sight

It was during his debates with John Kennedy that Richard Nixon began to understand the forces which television exerted upon the voting public. He had always understood the power held by the print media. The Los Angeles *Times*, for years during his races for representative and senator, was in bed so tightly with Nixon that they would not even mention his opposition's name. But when Dick went on television, looking seedy with a heavy beard and having his naturally shifty eyes beamed into the homes of millions of television viewers, the true impact of this relatively young medium began to hit home for the first time. There are those who say Nixon lost that election in 1960 because of television.

In 1960, Jesse Jackson was nineteen years old. He must have been paying attention to the fates of the powerbrokers because rarely has one individual used the medium—both print and visual—with the masterful strokes of a Jesse Jackson. Jesse has become as ingrained into our media consciousness as a Walter Cronkite or Dan Rather and not by accident.

An all-encompassing intelligence watching the nation for potential media hotshots might have turned a careful eye to Jackson's hometown of Greenville, South Carolina, during Jesse's early years. There was, at the time, something about the youngster that demanded attention, that called upon those around him to look at him and talk about him. It was a natural trait within the boy, something that would one day motivate television and newsreel cameras to focus on him.

Before Jesse had reached the age of ten, he was speaking in public, taking center stage and loving the hell out of it. He always pushed himself into the forefront, running for every school office, making every speech, trying to put himself into the limelight whenever possible. It would only be natural that he would love it when others did the work for him.

During his years with Martin Luther King, Jr., Jesse Jackson began to assume fame through association. When journalists were shooting photos of King, somehow the unknown Jesse Jackson would appear standing next to the great leader as though he belonged there. When there was a lull in a civil rights rally, Jesse would leap onto the stage and begin making a speech. He was good enough to pull it off, and people would not be incensed by his intrusion.

Those who worked with Jackson began to resent his leap toward the camera or at the journalist who was busy scribbling down his notes. They called Jackson a "hot dog" and a "media hound." They disliked the fact that others, with more seniority and longer, harder years behind them, were being pushed into the background while this young, aggressive black was stealing the show.

Being in the center, however, seemed to be a part of Jesse Jackson's nature. If he had felt called upon to stop, he probably couldn't have. It was second nature for him to leap at a camera, to make a speech, to shine when others retreated into a fog. Jackson has always been a showman, and most likely always will be.

Humility and humbleness were some of the earmarks of the early civil rights leaders. They were stern men, dedicated, and interested only in their causes. Their rhetoric was strong, but their presence as human beings was hidden behind the cloak of a sincere struggle. Jackson was different. He came on like a wild panther out of Harlem, and yet he spoke of nonviolence and brotherhood. He looked like an athlete, maybe even a movie star, but he could speak like a professor of economics or a street hustler from the Southside. He was a curiosity to the movement at first, but a likable and charismatic one. People seemed to be drawn to Jackson and he loved it.

The media and Jesse Jackson came together once and

for all on that terrible April evening in 1968 when an assassin's bullet struck down Martin Luther King, Jr. When King's aides had decided not to speak with the network newsmen who had gathered in the parking lot of the Lorraine Motel, Jesse Jackson took it upon himself to talk. The initial black voice heard by a grief-stricken and worried America was that of Jesse Jackson.

Later, when King's aides remained in virtual seclusion, Jackson was appearing on national television speaking about the tragic loss of King, but also laying the foundation for a direction for America's blacks. King's aides were tremendously angered over Jackson's assumption of the role as spokesman.

Being spokesman for the black race is a highly prized position. The reason: the United States and its press somehow assumes that the black people speak as a whole through only one man at any one given point in time. Why this situation exists, no one really understands, but it existed back in the time of Booker T. Washington and up through the era of Martin Luther King, Jr. A possible explanation of why this phenomenon exists might rest in the fact that the message which the black people of America has needed to put forth throughout the years has always been an unpleasant one. If the people are to listen, they want that message delivered to them by a constant voice, a voice which they can trust and rely upon. It may be the same psychology which keeps Walter Cronkite delivering the bad news of the world to millions of television viewers every night.

Other voices coming out of the black movement were

chaotic and often frightening. The Huey Newtons, the Elridge Cleavers and the Malcolm Xs spoke in a way which sent fear into the hearts of many. Their voices were not modulated with spirituality. Their message was one which white America could not tolerate. Martin Luther King's whole presence was benign. He was a friendly looking man, and his voice and phrasing were spiritual in origin. His message of nonviolent change was much easier to bear. So the press used King as the spokesman, the man who delivered the message for all blacks.

Unfair as it is, the "spokesman for the media" system did exist. Within minutes after the shooting of King, it appeared, at least on television and in the press, that Jesse Jackson was to become that new spokesman.

The style that would capture the attention of the media emerged quickly after King's death. Jesse Jackson had stood out among King and his aides, refusing to wear the customary dark suit and tie. Jesse preferred casual sweaters and the collegiate look. The press began to enjoy photographing the handsome youth whenever he would appear with King. Jackson just had that look, and that look will always get the cameras popping.

A year following King's death, Jackson once again scooped his fellow leaders during the Poor People's Campaign in Washington, D.C. The collection of poor people who had made the march under the banner of the SCLC and with the memory of Martin Luther King still fresh in their hearts turned into a rowdy bunch once they erected their camp in the nation's capital. Fights, rapes, robberies and general chaos were the order of the day, and it seemed that no one could calm the young black toughs who were the main cause of the disruption. Ralph Abernathy tried, and so did other leaders of the SCLC. No one could bring order to the group.

Then came Jesse. Jackson was a strider, an athlete and his mere physical presence seemed to bring the attention and respect of the crowd. Men who have a strong sense of purpose and a powerful body seem able to do that. Football great turned actor Jim Brown does it when he walks into a room. So did de Gaulle. Jesse Jackson, when he steps onto a podium, demands that the crowd turn their minds and ears toward him. When he faced the crowd at Resurrection City in Washington, he played his hand masterfully.

Jackson spoke to the young blacks as though he were challenging them on a street corner in Harlem. Jesse has always had a remarkable voice, and an actor's sense of using it. On that day in 1968, he lowered his voice, spoke mean and tough. He told the crowd that he could, "Walk that walk and talk that talk, too." The crowd listened, and they believed him. Jackson was playing the part of the street dude, bringing in a little muscle to the proceedings. The crowd quieted. Jackson organized the black gang members who had been causing much of the trouble to patrol the crowds as security police. The crisis had passed. During it all, the cameras were on Jackson, who played to them as well as the crowds. He was telling the media through his actions that he was one black able to relate directly to the "worst" elements of his own people. The white media and press sighed a heavy sigh of relief.

That ability of Jackson's to deal with all the diverse elements of the black movement was another factor which allowed Jackson to assume the title of media king for his people. Jackson constantly made it known that he respected the ideals of the Panthers, the Muslims, the SCLC (later after his split), CORE and the NAACP. He was always seeking the friendship and support of the leaders, and even though he often spoke negatively about these groups, he made sure the public understood that he respected them. Jackson was seeking to bridge the gap between the violent revolutionaries and the non-violent demonstrators, to stifle the gigantic split that was occurring within the movement.

This technique of publicly being able to relate to both the nonviolent SCLC and the very violent Black Panthers worked on another level with the white press. If the American people, and the media, thought that Jackson was something of a voice for all these groups, then Jackson's image of power would be extended. Jackson would appear to be the man who was holding back the hordes, keeping the revolution from boiling over. The implied threat would be that Jackson could, at any time, pull back and let the swarm settle upon white America. Although Jackson never directly spoke about this state of affairs, the implications were always there.

In Chicago, during Jackson's Saturday morning rallies for Operation Breadbasket, the voice of a Southern Baptist preacher boomed out across the airwaves. That voice belonged to Jesse Jackson, and it was a voice that stirred and moved his audiences. Jackson handled those shows as a preacher, using the chant, the cadence and the emotion filled question-response technique that so many tent preachers have found effective. Jackson's preaching over the radio was one of his most effective weapons. It held together his street organization, and at the same time gave notice to those he was attempting to change that he was active. It also gave him a nationwide platform (after the shows were picked up by a national network) to discuss and introduce new programs. But more important than any of the above was the fact that, for years, the morning radio shows kept Jackson directly and very emotionally in touch with black and white people throughout the country. Jackson understood well the need for constant exposure to create a feeling of trust and intimacy. He knew that if people understood that every Saturday morning he would be speaking with them again, those people would be hesitant in changing their allegiances during the week.

When Jackson travels on the road to speak at college campuses, local schools and meeting halls, he uses whatever media is available to him. From the way he dresses, whether in casual yet expensive Levis or in a "designer" three piece suit, to the way the stage is set, Jackson seems always conscious of the power of the visual. Early in his career, shortly after the death of King, Jackson staged a memorial rally for the great man at his Breadbasket headquarters in Chicago. When the mourners entered the auditorium, the first thing they saw was a huge portrait of Dr. King, with another large portrait of Jackson directly beneath him, as though Jackson were being handed the mantle of leadership by the slain leader from above. At his speaking engagements, Jackson will use the same kind of visual association to remind his audience who he is, and who he is in relation to Dr. King. With effective lighting, dramatic visuals and Jesse's own magical voice, his rallies are rarely unsuccessful. The man is a great showman and a fine speaker. The audiences react accordingly.

Jackson's understanding of the electronic media has always been astute. From that day in April when he stole the cameras and was the only member of the King party to appear on national television to the following morning when he flew back to Chicago to make an appearance on the Today Show, Jackson has never let an opportunity to present himself on television slide by. His television character is an ad man's dream.

Jackson is good-looking, but in a soft way. On the television screen, he possesses a boyish kind of charm, the same kind that Johnny Carson has used to entertain millions of viewers. That kind of alarm has always been a winner on television. Kennedy beat Nixon with it, and Jackson has beat his competition soundly using the same kind of charm. Jackson on television is much more than a mere charmer; he is also a man with a message. Jackson will never settle for boredom when he can say something that will create controversy. Using speech patterns that range from Harvard educated to Southern field worker, Jackson will shift and modulate according to his message. He will retreat into humble sensitivity, then strike back with the voice of a forceful revolutionary. He is never the same man twice on television, although many of his characters have made encore appearances.

This quality is exactly what television loves. Having Jesse Jackson on a talk show, the producer knows that he will not fail because of boredom. He knows that Jackson will always provide a good quote, an exciting piece of news or an inflammatory remark. Jesse always comes through, and he is always invited back.

Critics of Jackson call him a showboater and a hot dog, they resent Jackson's use and manipulations of the media. They do not understand that Jesse has learned what Kennedy knew, and what Nixon's men knew during the '68 and '72 campaigns—television sells products, and the American people are conditioned to buy those products. Sincere appeals for justice and humanity will not be heard by a public conditioned to laughter and entertainment. People want action, they want movement and they want glamor. The McGovern-Nixon race for the presidency in 1972 demonstrated the difference. McGovern was presented as a down home, softspoken and honest man. Quiet and sincere, he showed little action or movement. Nixon, on the other hand, never a colorful character, was nevertheless portrayed as a man on the move, as a president involved and determined. This was achieved through manipulative editing, where the men who put together the ads used fast cuts and quick paced shots. Nixon beat McGovern in a landslide that year. The television campaign which Nixon mounted contributed largely to his victory.

Jackson has watched and understood enough television to comprehend its workings. Jackson knows that movement is vital, or at least the illusion of movement. Jackson will move quickly in and out of a city, a demonstration, a rally, allowing just enough time for the television cameras to record his appearance. He used this technique at the Poor People's Campaign quite effectively, becoming the hero of a disastrous protest while Ralph Abernathy, who stayed during the entire campaign, became the goat.

Jackson also understands that much of the political sway of America during the seventies and into the eighties will come from television and the entertainment industry. Jackson has succeeded in surrounding himself with a large number of media people—mostly entertainers who remain capable of drawing the press to wherever they go. When they go to see Jackson, the press follows. People like Jim Brown, *Playboy* publisher Hugh Hefner, singer Nancy Wilson and Roberta Flack have lent their talents, as well as their fame, to Jackson's push for media exposure.

Although he is a favorite of the media, Jesse Jackson claims a love-hate relationship with the print media. He is constantly chiding and reprimanding reporters for misquoting him. He is also vehement when a reporter leaves his camp and ventures out onto the frontier of criticism. One woman reporter in Chicago, during the early days of Operation Breadbasket, wrote a column in one of the city's newspapers in which she criticized Jackson for his failure to follow through with his programs. She was also a regular member of the Saturday morning rallies. But the Saturday morning after her column appeared, she was booed loudly when she entered the hall. Jackson, standing at his pulpit, chastized her in front of the crowd.

Jackson will go out of his way to get to a reporter he feels has done him wrong; and he will often use whatever political or economic muscle he possesses to make sure that reporter knows where he stands. Jesse works very much like a president in the way he handles the press, with direct calls to journalists complaining of articles and pressure exerted upon them to correct their ways. Where Richard Nixon refused to talk to anyone with a typewriter, Jackson makes a point of keeping a relationship alive, even if it is a hate relationship. John Kennedy was very much the same. Both men understood the power of the press.

The national magazines have also treated Jackson well over the years. In 1970, Jackson made the cover of *Time* magazine, with a special edition dedicated to the black situation in America. In that issue, Jackson was heralded as the heir to Dr. King. Since then, almost every major magazine has run a full-length article on him. *Playboy* and *Penthouse* both gave him their interview spots. Every week, one can hardly pick up a magazine without some word about Jesse Jackson appearing inside.

With his announcement in November 1983 that he would seek the presidency, a whole new wave of media attention engulfed Jesse Jackson. The television networks; *Time, Newsweek, U.S. News & World Report*; and every major daily newspaper in America avidly followed Jackson's every move as the date of his announcement drew closer. He appeared on the cover of *Time* a full two months before officially announcing his candidacy.

Then in December of 1983, Lt. Robert Goodman, the black American airman, was shot down and captured by the Syrians. Jackson's bold move to win Goodman's release eclipsed all other media events—even the President's. Jesse Jackson's moral diplomacy has been attacked as another grandstanding ploy to attract media attention, but even President Ronald Reagan, who has the most to lose politically from Jackson's coup, admitted that "you don't quarrel with success." And Jesse Jackson's manipulation of the media throughout his career has been a major success.

Hollywood has also lent its special talents to the promotion and exposure of Jesse Jackson, who is as handsome and carefully packaged as any matinee idol. He made guest appearances on "The Lou Grant Show" playing himself, and has made the talk show circuit for years, from Dick Cavett and Tom Snyder to the "Phil Donahue Show." Jesse Jackson has capitalized on this national airtime to promote both his political views and, more importantly in image-conscious America, work his charismatic charms on the television audience.

Where has all this media attention gotten Jackson? For starters, it has made him the best known black man in America—a position that opened the door for his direct negotiations with President Assad of Syria. It has also served to create and mold an image of the man and candidate for the American public. A myth begins to build up around any famous celebrity, and our national politicians must be celebrities in order to survive the crush for media attention. Jesse Jackson's image has been carefully groomed to blend elements of hip, elegant, and handsome with his more serious attributes: energy, drive, and effectiveness. He is emerging among his own people as a legend, a cultural hero as well as a civil rights hero, a man who has been able to combine the hard-nosed aspects of politics with the flash and glitter of superstardom. He looks just as comfortable appearing in a Southside pool-room as he does sipping lime-flavored tonic water by the pool at Hugh Hefner's Los Angeles Playboy mansion. He is a star orbiting the skies over America, and when the media eye turns its attention toward him, people watch.

Jesse Jackson is the envy of politicians throughout the country. He is capable of moving faster and harder than the rest; he has garnered the headlines they sought; and he has appeared where they would like to appear. He is an independent media happening wherever he goes, always good for news and a lively quote. His flair, looks, and energy have propelled him into the limelight as only certain rock stars have been. The big difference lies in the fact that while some packaging of Jackson's message has taken place, it has not been gift-wrapped.

It is to Jesse Jackson's credit that within his spectrum as a national media star, he has not allowed his ''show'' to be innundated with hucksterism, or diluted by lack of purpose.

Other idealistic crusaders have started with the same pure motives, only to be devoured by the electronic monsters of the media. But for reasons of sheer brainpower, or instinct, Jesse Jackson has used the media without allowing it to eat him alive. Even though he is a star, he has refrained from acting like one. Instead, he has kept moving, pushing hard for his programs, pressuring the Democratic Party for his planks in the platform, maintaining his faith and belief even in the hypnotic eye of television. The traps still remain before him—and he has slipped a couple of times—but so far, Jesse Jackson has steered the true course between rocky shoals and sirens that cry out to seduce him.

Jesse Jackson being interviewed by the media during his 1988 campaign for the Democratic Party nomination.

Chapter 8

Jackson the Man

To many of the millions of blacks who have followed Jesse Jackson's every move, he has often come across as a high-flyer, a swinger who jets back and forth across the country, mingles with the beautiful people and is continually fighting off beautiful women. Jackson has done little to dispel that image. He dresses sharply and expensively, wearing custom-made buckskin and leather jackets, Italian boots and silk shirts and expensive three piece suits. When he walks onto a stage, everyone in the house knows that he is one black cat who has made it work.

The other segments of Jackson's life bear out his successful image. He drives late model, expensive cars and has, for many years, lived in a Tudor mansion on the Southside of Chicago. Jackson makes no pretense about the fact that he is doing well; he has never humbled himself and play at being poor. That is probably one of the man's greatest assets.

People who live on the poverty level, or somewhere above but without the luxuries of life, do not want to see other people suffering from the same plight. They do not want to listen to a man preaching about success and upward mobility who looks as though he'll be lucky to get a full meal after his speech is finished. What people want is a man who looks, acts and walks as if success is his, as if he is the shining example of his own words. That is precisely the role that Jesse Jackson fulfills. His audience sees a man who has it made, and they can relate to that. They see a man who speaks in a down to earth manner, digging at them to try harder, to straighten themselves out and make an effort with all of their weapons and talents. When Jackson speaks, people are affected because he is living proof of his own philosophy.

The swinging image of Jesse Jackson has followed him throughout his career. He has always been something of a ladies' man, at least in the eyes of the ladies. In high school, when Jesse was striding around the campus in Greenville, South Carolina, as the Big Man on Campus, his football coach warned him about the ladies. The coach knew that all the girls were fighting for the chance to get next to Jesse, and that Jesse might just be inundated by pretty women. That was something the coach did not want to see happen to his star quarterback. It might have affected the outcome of the season.

Jackson's popularity with the ladies has followed him throughout his career. Like Martin Luther King, Jr., the rumors have been persistent. Names like Nancy Wilson and Roberta Flack have been associated with the Reverend. But Jackson has denied that he has been involved with other women. He has told reporters that his friendships with Nancy Wilson, Roberta Flack and others were always based upon mutual respect and admiration, and not on sexual attraction.

The gossip mongers who try to build an image of Jesse Jackson as a coast to coast stud cite the fact that Jackson is on the road normally six days a week. Those who have traveled with him have seen the kind of reaction he causes in women. After one rally in a Southern city, the Jackson party was delayed at the airport because of rain and fog. A beautiful young woman approached Jackson and suggested that there might be a better place to spend a chilly, damp evening, namely, her hotel room. Jackson politely refused, telling the woman he was honored by her invitation.

Like most leaders who possess charisma, Jackson is continually under the microscope of the gossip writers. It is essential to human nature to speculate on the sex lives of the powerful, and Jackson is no exception to that rule. But we live in an era of higher sophistication, and our sensibilities toward that kind of thing have been modified. I can remember the incredible shock when it was first revealed that President Kennedy possessed an active libido. Some people were outraged, others let down. But for most, once the shock wore off, it didn't really matter that much. It came down essentially to the fact that what a man does with his private life is his own business, no matter who he is.

For the most part, Rev. Jesse Jackson has managed to keep his private life away from the public eye. And too, Jackson's public life is controversial enough to keep media tongues wagging.

Though maintaining a pace that would exhaust most jet-setters, Jackson is essentially a family man. His beautiful wife, Jacqueline, has been his woman for nearly twenty years. Together, they have raised a family of five children, all of them big Jesse Jackson fans. Those who have spent time with the Jackson family continually come away with nothing but praise and admiration for Jacqueline. She is a bright, literate woman with incredibly varied interests. Jesse met her initially as a political equal on the campus of A&T, and their relationship began over a discussion of politics and human rights.

During the initial months when Jesse began courting the beautiful coed, Jacqueline wasn't sure about her future husband. Like many others during those early days, she found Jesse impatient, audacious and loud. Loud enough, in fact, that his proposal of marriage was made in the midst of a crowd standing on a street corner. As Jacqueline was walking across the street in front of the group, Jesse yelled out to her that he was intending to marry her. She laughed, and so did Jesse's friends. But less than a year later, Jesse and Jacqueline took their vows in Jesse's home town of Greenville.

As public figures go, the Jackson couple has remained quiet and private throughout Jesse's stormy career. Jacqueline has lived in Chicago, in their gorgeous home, and has not traveled extensively. She maintains the household, pursuing interests which range from politics to astrology, while Jesse tours the country.

On Saturday afternoons, the Jackson household takes on the demeanor of a normal American home. Normal, that is, if one can ignore the continuing presence of armed bodyguards—part friend and part protector—who are always within earshot. Jackson comes home from his Saturday morning rallies and plays with his children, then wanders into the backyard to play a little basketball with his bodyguards. It is a time of peace and quiet for the leader, a time when he is able to assume the role of a normal father, at least for one day out of the week.

It is somewhat prophetic that Jesse Jackson, in many respects representative of a "super black man," is also afflicted by what is considered to be a "black man's disease." Jackson suffers from sickle cell anemia, a disease that afflicts many black Americans. Often the disease forces Jackson away from his incredible schedule and into the hospital for rest and treatment. Hospitalization has proven to be a relatively minor inconvenience as Jackson continues to handle his affairs, receiving visitors, processing paperwork, developing new programs and making plans for the future—all from his hospital bed.

Away from the hospital and home, Jesse Jackson has historically shouldered a daily schedule that would overtax a dozen men. He has maintained an eighteen hour day, logging hundreds of hours of flight time during the course of a year, moving from city to city, often state to state in a single day.

On a typical day the Jackson entourage has begun the

morning in Atlanta, Georgia, jetted nearly five hours to an evening speech out west in Los Angeles, then caught the "red eye" flight for New York to present his case before unnerved corporate executives.

A man in mercurial motion, Jackson, early on, had to come to grips with all the often negative vibrations that accompany the kind of fame and superstar stature that he has attained over the last 20 years, especially. And, as with all superstars, who live under a spotlight, at the mercy and whim of an adoring and sometimes fickle public, he has managed to weather even the most serious of storms, triggered by wrong words at the wrong time, with the media amplifying and repeating the mental error for the entertainment of the public. He has become a superstar who must deal with all of the problems of someone who literally has lost all control of his privacy—unlike Ralph Ellison's "Invisible Man," Jackson has become all too "visible."

One of Jackson's unique and most valuable qualities has been his powers as, not simply an orator capable of wooing masses, but as a communicator, able to deal one-on-one with people as diverse as a midwestern farmer and an urban welfare family.

Unlike many politicians who hone their talents and philosophies in the sometimes thin air of academe, Jackson began his public career as a man of the people, a leader sensitive to, and one with, the needs of the poor, the disadvantaged, the disenfranchised. A front line soldier in the early Civil Rights and Poor People's Campaigns, Jackson has the rep of a seasoned veteran in the war, not only against racism, but against poverty that crosses all racial, cultural and age groupings. Since his earliest days in the struggle for civil rights, Jackson has been laying the groundwork and building the foundation for what has become the Rainbow Coalition, a political machine fueled and manned by the people who needed him and his stature most of all.

Few men possess the talent, insight or ability of a Jesse Jackson to come off as one of the boys. When he has had to deal with black street gangs, he has come off as a man tougher than they are. When he had to deal with Richard Daley's thugs, Jackson organized black gang members and came off as a nearly violent revolutionary. When Jackson has had to walk into the corporate meeting rooms of some of the nation's most powerful conglomerates, he has come off as a sharp, shrewd businessman. When Jackson has found it necessary to place himself in the role of a hip, fun-loving *nouveau riche*, he has been able to do that. Some people have objected to Jackson's man-for-all-seasons personality, calling him a chameleon. But Jesse's talent has allowed him to invade rooms where others would have never gained admittance. It has allowed him to speak with men who have the power to change things. And it has allowed him to promote his programs outside the normal channels.

This talent has also allowed Jackson to move within the circles of power of the black movement itself. He has been able to speak with and deal with all facets of the revolutionary, violent and religious divisions within the movement. He is the one man who has been capable of meeting underground with the Black Panthers, then walking across the street and spending his afternoon with the Black

Muslims.

The chameleon aspect of Jackson's personality may irritate a lot of people, but Jackson has used it successfully.

Beneath the glitter and fame of Jesse Jackson lies a man who is basically a conservative. Jackson does not smoke, drink or take drugs, and he looks down upon people who do. He considers the moral decay of American society a force to be reckoned with. "Many of us allow our children to eat junk, watch junk, listen to junk, talk junk, play with junk, and then we're surprised when they come out to be social junkies." Jackson's attitude toward American society is summed up in the above words. He firmly believes in traditional morality, in a morality that defines the individual by his actions and deeds. He sees the forces at loose in this nation as forces that are undermining the abilities of everyone, but much more the blacks. Jackson feels that black children have farther to go, and thus must overcome the moral decay of a society which is basically white. Jackson, like so many other black religious leaders, has come to terms with white society in that they feel whites have gotten there, become bored by their gains and are now slipping into a moral abyss. His message to blacks is one of rising out of the conditions which have not only been imposed on them by injustice, but also those which have resulted from a nationwide decay of morality. "If we are to lift ourselves out of this morass," Jackson says, "we must shift our sights from the superficial to the sacrificial."

Jackson is, and has always been, accessible, the key to his man of the people status, even though he is, financially, more on a par with the inaccessible rich.

Unlike many leaders who seek change, Jesse Jackson boasts a record of personal success, even while "crying poor" for the deserving of this nation. He is a wealthy man, he has opened the doors to the world of the white man for himself. He is a successful businessman, a success within the social world and a media giant. His needs are anything but personal. There is no ego within Jesse Jackson that says he must climb higher into the party life of the white man. Richard Nixon was a perfect example of a man who gained power, and seemed to need that power in order to be accepted by those circles which had always been closed off to him. Nixon's hatred of the Kennedys was based on this unfulfilled need. He had always felt left out, rejected. His climb into the White House may have very well been motivated by his need to join the circles of the elite. But Nixon really never had a program, never really had a goal which went beyond his own personal needs. That was his failing, and that was why he was so corruptible. Jesse Jackson, because of his own personal success, both monetarily and as a "beautiful person," has eliminated those personal needs. He has completed an agenda of personal success and established himself.

Instead of Jackson eyeing the white world as a promising city of splendor, he is now able to look upon it from a point of equality. He can buy what the white man buys, go where the white man goes and live a life as wild and hedonistic as the white—if he chooses. Jackson chooses to look with a qualitative eye on the world of whites, and what that world is doing to its citizens.

Television, music and drugs; sex and violence; all the

earmarks of a degenerating society are present. Jackson talks about them, and issues a warning to his people about them. He knows that what black children are seeing on television is controlled by whites. If there are blacks involved, they are just as degenerate in their focus as the white man. Jackson is telling everyone that an entire generation is coming up mired in the worlds of idiocy, mindlessness and depravity. His traditional morality is speaking out against this world.

It is interesting that President Jimmy Carter, in the early summer of 1979, came out with the same message that Jackson has been delivering for the last seven years. Carter said that the country was in a state of "moral crisis" because of its emphasis on sex, drugs and violence. He called for the nation to rearm itself morally, and to shake off the direction which is now plunging it into a moral abyss. It is the same message that Jackson delivers. But it is a message which, when delivered by Jackson, carries more weight.

As a human being, Jesse Jackson is a driven man. He does not stop. His world is a world of movement, effect and counterpunch. He is possessed by a crusade and by the action which that crusade provides. He is a man of unlimited energy, tremendous vision and shrewd powers of the mind which allow him to create that vision into a reality. Beneath the spiritual heart and the goal-oriented mind there is another Jesse Jackson who seems to have a real, pragmatic grasp on his position.

One evening a few years ago, a local Chicago movement worker saw Jesse Jackson emerging from a movie theater. The worker complained that while there was still so much suffering within the black community it was unfair and shallow for Jesse Jackson to waste time watching a piece of screen fiction. Jackson attacked. He told the press that it was ridiculous for them to assume that because he was Jesse Jackson, that he should be denied any of the pleasures which life has to offer. What he was saying, in essence, was that he was a human being, too, and that just because he was a black man fighting for justice for his people, was not a reason for him to entirely sacrifice his life. The moral sense within Jackson is powerful, and he asks his followers to seek a higher moral level. But in so doing, he walks the fine line. Jackson does not ask his people to become saints, to abstain completely. He asks them to achieve a balance, to walk a steady road between pleasure and sacrifice. His message, when looked at under the magnified eye of society as a whole, is pragmatic and filled with common sense. It is much less a spiritual message than a simple word to the wise.

Jesse Jackson has achieved what many men only dream about. He rides in limousines, lives elegantly, and is worshipped by millions of people. Within the context of his fame, Jesse Jackson never stops. He does not let the light of fame blind him to his role and the effect that can have on the destiny of millions of people.

In 1973, Jackson's home town of Greenville, South Carolina, threw him a welcome home party. Jesse Jackson had become Greenville's most famous son, and the Southern town went all out to welcome Jesse home.

The return to Greenville must have seemed like a dream come true. Through the progress of the civil rights movement, the town had become fully integrated. Hotels which had refused service to blacks only a decade or so before now opened their doors with a welcome sign to blacks who gathered for the special day. Neighborhoods which had been formerly segregated now housed black families living alongside white families.

The town of Greenville that day had turned out to pay its respects and to honor Jesse Jackson. And the world joined them. Journalists from the far reaches of the globe congregated in the Southern town; politicians, entertainers and sports heroes arrived to attend the banquet given in Jackson's honor. It seemed that almost everyone who was anyone had traveled to Greenville in order to attend.

Jesse Jackson flew into town a hero. He was remembered there, and the people who watched him grow up came out to greet him. Jackson had come home. He had brought the world with him. It was a moment that everyone who has ever wished to be somebody has dreamed of. Every man, during his lifetime, has hoped that someday all those he knew during the time when he was a ''nobody'' would stand and applaud the person he had become. That one moment would make up for all of the abuse, all of the pain, all of the heartache of trying to reach manhood. For Jesse Jackson, the moment must have been especially sweet. His youth had been tainted by his birth to an unwed mother. The calls of ''bastard'' had rung through his ears more than once. His childhood in Greenville had been a struggle to assert himself, to establish an identity.

Now he was coming home, telling everyone just by his presence that he had, indeed, become somebody. The town was at his feet, offering itself to Jesse Jackson as only he could have dreamed it would during his early years.

Parades, demonstrations and banquets were held to honor the returning hero. The mayor, Jackson's former schoolteachers and coaches, and those who had known him, offered to speak. Everyone wanted to be a part of the homecoming.

At the large banquet held shortly after his arrival, Jackson was honored in high style. Speeches ranged long into the evening, with friends and admirers telling the young black leader that he was "good for America" and "America's hope."

Sitting on the dais, watching those who had once watched him, must have given Jackson an incredible sense of justification. He must have felt a certain, "I told you so," toward these people. And he must have felt an incredible satisfaction that evening.

Any other man might have been satisfied to bathe in the glory of his moment of triumph, but not Jesse Jackson. When he rose to speak, there was thunderous applause. Jackson thanked everyone, and told them how the town of Greenville had always been his "bridge over troubled waters." Then, without warning, Jackson shocked everyone by launching into an impassioned speech about the work left to be done. As far as the people gathered there were concerned, this was a night to rest on laurels, a night to sit back with fine food and drink and bathe in the glory of past deeds. But for Jesse Jackson, it was a night to continue his push toward the light. He would not be content with sitting back watching the men and women step to the speaker's platform and toast him. He would use the opportunity as a vehicle, knowing that the press was there and that his words would reach out across the globe.

The Greenville homecoming for Jesse Jackson provided a good insight into the man. It allowed his almost cold directness to emerge. It said to many that there was really no way to buy this enigmatic man off. It said to people that Jesse Jackson's ego was firmly under control, and that he maintained his focus on his goals at all times. Some of the gathering were shocked and dismayed by Jackson's speech that night, feeling that it was out of place considering the circumstances. For those who knew Jackson well, the speech came as no surprise. Jackson loved the gesture on the part of his friends and the townspeople of Greenville, but he also saw the opportunity which that gesture provided him. He took that opportunity, seizing the moment and pushing ahead. As a human being, that seems to be the quality most consistent within Jackson. He is undoubtedly an opportunist, but fortunately, he is one who is working toward the positive. There are many people in this country who are grateful for that fact.

Chapter 9

Run, Jesse, Run

"If you want somebody to feed the hungry, here am I. Send me! If you want someone to clothe the naked, here am I. Send me! If you want someone who can pull this nation together—black, white, brown, old, young—here am I. Send me!"

And the crowds in Chicago and Atlanta and Louisville, and Los Angeles and New York and Dallas, respond to Jesse Jackson with their chant: "Run, Jesse, run! Run, Jesse, run!"

In November, 1983, at the Washington, D.C. Convention Center, Jesse Jackson made it official that he would seek the Democratic Party's nomination for President of the United States. The long wait was over, the guesswork and predictions by political pundits no longer mattered, because Jesse had weighed all the options and decided to run. Sighs of relief from supporters were met with those of dismay from other Democratic candidates and the campaign staff of Ronald Reagan. Jesse Jackson would upset the balance of power so carefully created by the established powers, Jesse Jackson would be a volatile element they hadn't fully prepared for, Jesse Jackson would change the way the political game was played in America—possibly forever.

During the early days of Jackson's career, when he was still with SCLC and Dr. King, Jackson began building a power base with its roots planted firmly within the movement. At that time, he began collecting ministers and preachers, black leaders who would support him after the death of Dr. King. Within the movement itself, however, Jackson was a divisive factor, and found it difficult to establish a base of allegiance with other movement leaders. Jealousy, envy, and irritation were displayed by the black power brokers at the time of Jesse Jackson's assumption to the role of King's heir. Those wounds, beginning with the schism between Jackson and Ralph Abernathy, were still in evidence as Jesse Jackson made his run for the highest office in the land. Prominent leaders such as Mayor Coleman Young of Detroit, Mayor Andrew Young of Atlanta, Mayor Tom Bradley of Los Angeles, Benjamin Hooks of the NAACP, and even Dr. King's widow, Coretta, failed to step forward in support of Jesse Jackson's bid for the Presidency.

Black leaders feared that Jesse's candidacy might

weaken the Democrats' chances of unseating Ronald Reagan, the number one priority for all black leaders, including Jackson. They feared Jesse would take votes away from Walter "Fritz" Mondale, whose voting record as U.S. Senator and Vice President on black and civil rights issues was sterling.

Mondale was especially vulnerable to losing votes in the South, where a large proportion of black votes are cast, and where a voter registration drive for additional black votes was in full swing. Jesse Jackson's drawing power could swing some Southern states toward a rival Democratic candidate, John Glenn, whose conservative voting record in Congress branded him a Republican in Democratic clothing. Glenn consistently supported Ronald Reagan's programs to cut social programs and boost the defense budget.

But Jesse Jackson said he was not in the race to influence the primaries toward one candidate or the other; he was in the race to win. And though few give him any chance whatsoever to actually win the Democratic nomination, Jackson vowed his voice would be heard at the Convention. To the relief of the Democratic leadership, Jesse also pledged not to run as a third party candidate should he lose the Democratic nomination—a divisive strategy that would have most certainly assured Ronald Reagan his second term in office. As it turned out, it made little difference—except for Jackson's reputation among party leadership.

The black movement after Martin Luther King's assassination began losing its foothold of power in the United States. The SCLC lost in repeated moves to integrate and deal in power brokerage in Chicago. Eventually the SCLC withdrew, concentrating its efforts in the South, leaving Jesse Jackson alone in the North with the Black Panthers, CORE, the Black Muslims, and other radical groups.

Having Chicago virtually to himself, especially after the police there systematically wiped out the leadership of the Panthers, Jesse Jackson began building his own political machine, one that would grow in power great enough to ultimately topple Richard Daley himself. Jesse Jackson started his move toward power in 1966 with economic issues, using the power of black politics to open doors to black capitalism. His system, Operation Breadbasket, of economic boycott against white-owned businesses that discriminated, pitted him against giants such as A&P food markets and Coca-Cola. The system worked, and Operation Breadbasket emerged victorious time after time. Soon Jackson was responsible for the great success of many black businessmen. At the same time he began moving into the corporate chambers of some of America's largest businesses, dealing with the boards of directors as though he were one of them. Jackson became so proficient at wheeling and dealing with the corporate world that one top executive was known to have offered Jesse *anything* he wanted to join the company.

Thus Jackson began cultivating the business world. His movements within their circle showed him to be an astute, shrewd negotiator, and gained him the respect of America's corporate world.

After Dr. King's death, Jesse Jackson slowly assumed the role as leader and spokesman for the movement. With his economic base solidly in position and flourishing, Jesse set his sights on the power of politics. He ran for mayor and lost, but fought Richard Daley on the floor of the Democratic Convention and won, unseating the host city's mayor and his delegation. He later gave the opening address at the Democratic Convention in New York. The early seventies gave Jackson a clear visibility among the American people. His name was becoming a household word, and he was viewed as a colorful and unusual politician.

Experts laughed at Jackson's political maneuvers. What bothered them most was Jackson's shifting back and forth between the Democratic and Republican Parties. Jackson played them both against the middle, and would shift allegiance depending upon which Party was willing to support his programs. So, at one point, the Democrats thought they had Jackson and his voting bloc sewn up, but in typically unpredictable fashion, Jesse turned his back when they did not deliver and cast his allegiance with the Republicans. Back in those days Jackson was laughable as a political candidate, but as a power broker with the thrust of the black movement behind him, Jesse Jackson was a force to be reckoned with.

With the Watergate scandal and Nixon's resignation, Americans began looking at their politicians with a certain curiosity. Nixon had shown the potential for corruption within the system, and so had given those who fought their battles outside the system a certain credibility. A man such as Jesse Jackson, who had never participated directly within the system, was trusted more than the elected officials themselves.

It was probably best for Jesse Jackson that he did not

win his race for mayor, or that he had not been seduced into running for other offices. Jackson has maintained an individuality separate from the political mainstream throughout his career, and this separation has most likely benefited his public image. He remains, to this day, a political maverick. Judging by what the American people's attitude toward politicians has become, Jackson's non-political base probably has provided him with another incredibly strong foundation.

On another level, Jesse Jackson has managed to create a following of grass roots supporters as a result of his programs and his speeches. Throughout the country, black people have gathered in an almost worshipful sense when Jesse Jackson appears to make a speech. His Southern, down-home style of preaching electrifies his listeners. His in-person charisma is unequaled by any other major public figure in the nation. He is the kind of speaker who can raise crowds to a frenzy, using the cadences of the old tent revivalists. He is also the kind of man who strikes at the center of an issue and provides people with a direct goal. His PUSH-Excel program was a perfect example of this power. He provided people with a program which they could adhere to, and affected hundreds of thousands of children and their parents. Even though many critics complained that Jackson's program for uplifting the educational levels of blacks was simple-minded and without true substance, the fact remains that Jackson brought together huge groups of people to act together in the same manner, to strive for a goal.

The people, then, represent another huge power base which Jesse Jackson cultivated and developed over the years. He is tremendously popular with blacks, and very popular with whites as well. The educators, liberals, and businessmen confronted with the tricky problem of doing business within the black inner cities all support Jackson.

Another area where Jackson has shone brightly is that of the media. He's played the media for all its worth, always providing news and always making it. He has managed to become the most written about, talked about and photographed black man of the last two decades.

In Jackson's corner are many of the men and women who *are* the media. The reporters, television commentators, and gossip columnists all seem to enjoy Jesse Jackson and his style. His color, his flair, his energy all serve to make their jobs easier. They've watched him and written about him for years, and although many criticize him, there is always a continuing feeling of respect and admiration for the man. So, sitting in Jesse Jackson's corner is much of the national media, one of the most powerful forces in America.

Along with the other elements of society who seem to have gathered behind Jesse Jackson is the entertainment industry. Actors, athletes and writers congregate around the Reverend with unabashed loyalty. Jackson is one of them, especially among the young blacks who are making it big in the entertainment field. The tone has shifted within films, records and television since the days of Stepin Fetchit and Amos 'n Andy. The blacks who work in the industry today are not as fearful of being aggressively male as were their counterparts a decade or two ago. Jackson's aggressive maleness intrigues and captures them. It is somewhat like a new brotherhood of black men emerging on the scene: men who swagger, men who boast, men who create and make news. Martin Luther King, Jr., and the men before him were in a much trickier position and had to remain subdued in order to achieve their goals. This is not true today. The black men on the forefront can afford to let go a little, to be as colorful as well as strong. People like Lou Gossett, Jr. and Ossie Davis are men who can relate to Jackson, not merely as a spiritual leader, but as a comrade in arms in a fight to change the conditions not only of the black man but all citizens in America. There is a new swagger to the movement, a new boldness that is refreshing and positive. Jesse Jackson seems to epitomize that new direction.

Within the political system in America are a great number of politicians who are supportive of Jesse Jackson. He seems to be able to make men understand him, to speak their language. He has walked out of meetings where cynical politicians sat at a long table listening to him, ready to vote against him. Yet, Jackson has emerged victorious. Why? Comments on Jackson's effectiveness with the political animal range from his being able to outpower them to the fact that Jackson will win them over with love. Jackson is a player and always has been. His savvy is that of the street, and he carries that shrewdness wherever he goes. In conference and debate, he goes for the jugular, whether that be in the heart, the mind or the posterior. Politicians respect that in a man. They pay attention to a man who can come in and play their games of persuasion better than they can. Jackson is an ultimate persuader. More than one stone-faced gentleman with power has emerged from a meeting with Jesse Jackson saying that he has personally gone through a change, that he has seen the light. Jackson takes the preacher with him wherever he goes, and in the arena of politics, he is extremely effective.

Within the continental United States, Jesse Jackson has a power base that is literally second to none within the scope of black leaders; it is a power base comparable to that of strong white politicians. Jackson is capable of sweeping across the nation and receiving press coverage, good audience response, and cooperation no matter where he goes. There are very few men in this country who can claim that same kind of extended base and support.

During the summer of 1979 Jesse Jackson arrived in South Africa amidst the turmoil of that country's racial situation to extend his operations. Previously, during the mid-seventies, Jackson had traveled to Ethiopia and other African nations presumably to create business between those nations and black businessmen in America. His missions of commerce were fairly well received, and Jackson managed to open a few doors of trade between the African continent and the North American continent. But a more recent voyage into the heart of South African apartheid was something different.

Speaking in front of 10,000 of that nation's blacks, Jackson revved up his Southern preacher's voice and began sermonizing as he did on his Saturday morning broadcasts out of Chicago. "Apartheid is violence by definition," Jackson shouted. "It rules on fears and lies, it violates free will, burns the body, limits the mind. Its ultimate sin is that it divides the church." The crowd of South African blacks cheered and called out to him much the same way a crowd in Atlanta would. Jackson, standing before them in a zebra-skin cloak and hat, wowed them with his rhetoric, and brought them to their feet more than once with declarations such as: "Apartheid is worse than Hitler."

The trip to South Africa was an experiment in broadening Jackson's territory of influence. He spent twelve days touring the country, visiting American-owned corporations there and advising those corporations to hire more blacks in management and executive positions. Jackson also took a stand on international boxing by coming out against an upcoming match between Pretoria's Gerrie Coetzee and America's John Tate. Jackson said that if Tate fought in South Africa, he would be a "traitor to his people." The two-week tour raised the eyebrows of many of South Africa's leaders, and, as usual, Jackson elicited all manner of reactions from the host country. He was cited as being a cynical manipulator "more interested in running for Congress than helping his people," called a "Communist," and the government resented his comments and his visit. They felt strongly that he had no business coming to South Africa and condemning the progress of that country when "there were thousands of blacks . . . living in deplorable conditions" in America.

And yet, thousands upon thousands of black workers came out to see the irrepressible Jesse Jackson, and they responded to him as though he were a folk hero come alive. The reaction to his "I am somebody" call for self-respect was overwhelming. The people loved him, the power structure hated him. A typical day in the life of Jesse Jackson.

The question remains, however, as to why Jesse Jackson felt called upon to go into that bastion of apartheid, where the racial question sits like a keg of dynamite with a lit fuse. The answer may rest in Jesse Jackson's drive to establish his name on a world-wide basis, to extend his reach beyond the continental United States. The reasons he wanted to do this at this time were many, and terribly complex. Basically, it rested within the theory that the Third World countries, on the rise throughout the world and sitting on incredible resources, both natural and human, would sometime in the near future determine much of the political balance of the superpowers. We had already experienced this phenomenon with the OPEC nations and their effect on the world balance. Jackson, always intuitive to future power plays, was most likely setting his sights on the rising black class in South Africa, that majority of humanity who, by destiny of their numbers, would someday soon rule that nation.

America had an incredible array of corporate interests in South Africa, and as a minister of goodwill from America into South Africa, Jesse Jackson was a perfect choice. He was in a position to speak directly to the people, condemn the racism, and yet maintain a foothold within the business community. It was the same tactic which Jackson used in dealing with Richard Daley's Chicago. He made no attempt to speak directly to the machine until he had established some momentum within the black business world. It was quite possible that Jackson was attempting to do the same thing in Africa.

Moving his influence outside the United States, and securing a foothold through commerce, would give

Jackson a potential of power rarely seen by a leader of people. By going directly to the populace, Jackson was undercutting the governments and the politics of compromise. By bringing with him his record for corporate success, he was structuring a monetary stronghold which would and did speak louder than words.

There had been many cases where black leaders had gone to the roots, so to speak. Back to Africa was a cry of the sixties, and men like Ron Karenga were effective in pushing for a move back to the mother continent. But never had the movement seen one of its leaders attempting to deal with Africa as an emerging power of economic and natural resources. This, apparently, Jesse Jackson was starting to do. As usual, he angered the power structure and created chaos among the leaders with regards to himself.

So Jesse Jackson was succeeding in structuring a worldwide power base for himself and his programs, a base of operations that stretched across the oceans and into the Third World countries. There were those who felt that this move was only an inevitable step in a master plan conceived and directed by the brilliant leader in order to someday assume the highest office in the land, that of the Presidency.

The scenario, according to those who believed in its existence, went something like this: Jesse Jackson begins outside the realm of politics, and establishes a base of operations among blacks. At the same time, he woos and wins the loyalty of big business by dealing with them on a give-and-take basis, establishing himself as a man who can handle himself in the high-powered world of corporate compromise. Meanwhile, Jackson woos and wins over the media, striking out as a fanciful, colorful personality without ever going too far overboard. With extensive media coverage, Jackson becomes the best known black man in America. The scenario continues with Jackson pursuing an entire generation of young blacks through his operation PUSH-Excel. The theory here becomes extremely interesting.

The cynics believed that PUSH-Excel was little more than an attempt on the part of Jesse Jackson to gain control of an entire generation. Critics of the program continually cited Jackson for his "rules" and the manner in which he handled audiences at PUSH-Excel rallies. One critic berated Jackson for the emphasis which Jackson placed on dress codes in high schools. At one rally, Jackson refused to speak until all the males in the audience removed their hats. The critic felt that Jackson was not so much interested in helping these kids advance their own education as he was in "training" the children to follow his orders. Other critics cited the mass chanting and mass audience response of the young to Jackson when he spoke, following his calls of "I am somebody" with an almost hysterical reverence. Jackson told these kids to turn off their televisions, their radios, and their record players, and to open their books. But, was he also telling them to close their minds to all leaders but himself? Was Jackson attempting to train a generation which, in four or five years, would be of voting age, to follow him with a fanatical reverence? There were some critics who believed this to be true.

The scenario continued. By 1984 Jackson had a newly

registered army of black voters behind him, ready to sweep him into office—or so goes the scenario.

Jesse Jackson has a newly registered army of black voters, but it probably won't be enough to elect him President. What it will do is change the face of American politics, not merely for this one election, but for generations to come. And in the long run, that may be more important to black power politics than Jesse Jackson in the White House.

His candidacy quickly changed the campaign strategies of Walter Mondale and John Glenn. Both were appealing heavily to black voters for support, especially in the Southern states. Even Ronald Reagan had tossed a few bones toward the black vote in hopes of preventing the Democratic nominee from sweeping the black vote.

Why all this sudden flurry of interest in black voting power? Jesse Jackson had pushed for voter registration for years, but his official candidacy had galvanized the grass roots organizers, and nearly all black civil rights organizations—even the ones headed by Jackson's enemies—made the registration of black voters their number one priority for the 1984 election. The will to topple Ronald Reagan, coupled with a groundswell of support for Jesse Jackson, made 1983 the most successful year for voter registration since the Civil Rights Voting Act was passed. Two million new black voters signed up in 1983 alone, and there will be more before the November elections.

Jesse Jackson had led the fight with a traveling show that toured the country like a voter registration revival meeting. "There's a freedom train a-coming!" he shouted.

"But you got to be registered to ride. Get on board! Get on board!"

He went to schools, churches, shopping malls, military bases (where a huge proportion of black servicemen signed up and obtained absentee ballots), and anywhere a crowd could be raised. He exhorted his flock to register, then register their friends and neighbors. "When you run, the masses register and vote," he promised. "When you run, you put your program on the front burner." Then he warned, "If you run, you might lose. But if you don't run, you're guaranteed to lose!"

He said that there could be 46,000 more black elected officials on the state, local, and national levels—if only blacks would register and vote. He told them there was a potential for seven million more black voters, and that the system could work if black politicians learned to work the system. He turned them from the "Burn, baby, burn" slogans of the '60s to the "Learn, baby, learn" of his PUSH-Excel programs, and rallied the crowd by leading the chant: "Run, Jesse, run!"

With a potential three million more black votes in 1984 than there were in the 1980 elections, mainstream politics suddenly sat up and took notice of issues directly affecting black voters. A 25 percent increase in black registration would affect not only the 1984 election but the balance of power in politics on state, local, and national levels for years to come.

In addition to registering new black voters, Jesse Jackson's run for the Presidency had positive results for other minorities as well. For Jackson saw his campaign as a "Rainbow Coalition" of blacks, Hispanics, Orientals, women, human rights activists, and other minority groups left outside mainstream politicians' concerns. He had worked to force a coalition of the rejected and disenfranchised.

He reminded audiences that he, too, experienced the depression of rejection: "When I was in my mother's belly, no father to give me a name, they called me bastard and rejected me." He has revealed in his own life that there is a way out of depression, a way to the end of the rainbow, with his Rainbow Coalition. "My experience in life," he said, "has been that one must struggle to turn adversity to advantage. One way to overcome your oppressor is to outdistance him."

"Run, Jesse, run! Run, Jesse, run!" the people shouted in response.

In addition to fulfilling his own personal goals, and in addition to the benefits his own candidacy would gain from the addition of so many new black voters, there was a longer range, more idealistic side to Jesse Jackson's run for the White House. By entering the arena first, he blazed a new trail for generations of black politicians to come. "My running," Jackson said, "will stimulate thousands to run, it will make millions register. If we can get our share of legislators, mayors, sheriffs, school board members, tax collectors, and dog catchers, we can live with whoever is in the White House." And he knew that for black voters to remain interested in politics, there must be some victories—and once there were victories, the black voter would become involved in the process over and over again. That was crucial in the long-range strategy of capturing some of those 46,000 offices that Jackson figured should be occupied by black politicians.

By running, Jackson reinforced the litany of catch phrases, slogans, and jingles that were created around his image—he put teeth into the chant he led at young people's rallies. "I am somebody!" he urged kids to shout. At first only a few embarrassed voices would respond, but he built the rhythm of the chant and slowly won them over to the idea of shouting it out loud and clear and proud. "I may be on welfare ... " he coaxed, "but I *am* somebody! I may be uneducated ... but I AM somebody! I may be hungry ... but I AM SOMEBODY! I may have lost hope ... " and they were with him, standing, shouting, "I AM SOMEBODY!"

Jesse Jackson lost in his first bid for the Presidency, but he had proven that he was somebody. And he had instilled hope in millions of the hopeless that they can be somebody, too.

With an oddly paternalistic attitude, the Democratic Party leadership complained of the hope Jesse Jackson brought to black voters. They worried, they said, that when Jesse lost, that black voters will be disillusioned, bitter, despondent, and apathetic toward a white Democratic nominee. Jesse Jackson has listened with patience to such condescending charges, then explained calmly that black voters are no less sophisticated than white voters, and if there is a candidate who speaks to the issues that concern blacks, they will vote for that candidate whether black, white, or any other color.

In addition to shaking up the Democratic Party, and in addition to the flash of style he had added to the 1984 Presidential campaign, Jesse Jackson also had a platform, a plan of action, should he by some miracle be elected.

This is where Jesse Jackson stood on the major domestic and international issues:

Economics He believed in capitalism, and through programs like Operation Breadbasket, had seen it work for the disadvantaged. He believed capitalism could work, but it must work for all people, not just a privileged few .

Jobs Jesse Jackson proposed full employment with job training for all. He opposed Reaganomics and the trickle-down theory, preferring demand-side economics that work from the bottom-up.

Middle East He would protect Israel's right to exist while pursuing self-determination and a homeland for the Palestinians. He would encourage dialogue with the PLO.

Nuclear weapons He supported top-level meetings with the Soviets to limit and reduce nuclear arms. He would never endanger the nation's security, he said, but added that it was time to start taking some risks for peace.

Central America He opposed supporting the big landowners over the poor people and the church in El Salvador. He would tie any future aid to that country on improvements in their human rights record. He would cancel support to the rebel troops in Nicaragua, and charged the Reagan Administration with covertly trying to overthrow the Nicaraguan government.

Military He would freeze the military budget at present levels, reduce the number of U.S. troops in Europe, and scrap the B-1 bomber program along with the MX and nerve gas.

Civil rights He would strengthen and enforce federal laws to protect the civil rights of minority groups, women, workers, and the poor. He would place particular emphasis on voting rights, charging the Democratic Party with violating the law, and the Republicans with refusing to enforce the law.

South Africa He pointed out the hypocrisy of Americans defining democracy at home as majority rule, while it was defined as minority rule in South Africa.

He called his platform the "New Course," an obvious reference to Roosevelt's New Deal, and it was a course guided by Jackson's deep commitment to moral choices. A certain consistency was evident in his policy statements. It would not be fair to support Israel's right to exist while denying the Palestinians theirs. It was not right for the Soviets to invade Afghanistan, but neither was it morally right for the United States to invade Grenada. We should not covertly try to overthrow an elected government in Nicaragua, nor should we support South Africa's minority rule.

Some complained of Jackson's idealism, pointing out a more pragmatic approach of rewarding our friends and punishing our enemies as more appropriate policy for a world power. But Jesse Jackson argued that only by setting an example, living by our own ideals, could the United States effectively influence world politics.

His positions sometimes sounded closer to a preacher's way of viewing the world than a politician's, but then that's why he had been called a prophet on a political mission.

Jesse Jackson believed he would win the Democratic Party's nomination for President and go on to defeat Ronald Reagan in November. Despite all the evidence to the contrary, Jesse Jackson believed he would be President of the United States. "You see," he explained, "I really believe I was born to be a leader."

"Run, Jesse, run!" they shouted.

Chapter 10

The Moral Pilgrimage

One month after Jesse Jackson announced his candidacy for President in Washington, D.C., a U.S. Navy fighter-bomber was shot down over Lebanon while on a reconnaissance flight over Syrian troop positions. The pilot was killed, and the navigator-bombardier, Lt. Robert O. Goodman, Jr., was taken as a prisoner-of-war. It would prove to be the most startling development in the 1984 campaign, and Jesse Jackson would emerge the hero.

Defying his President, the U.S. State Department, and many of his own advisors, Jesse Jackson undertook a personal diplomatic mission to free the captured American flyer. He was criticized by the press as making a headline-grabbing gesture that would do nothing to help Lt. Goodman's cause, and he was denounced privately by other Democratic candidates as grandstanding in a hopeless cause. But Jesse Jackson did not undertake his mission to Syria merely to advance his own political position, he made the moral pilgrimage out of frustration with Ronald Reagan and his Administration's failure to negotiate with the Syrians over Goodman's release. Jesse Jackson felt the black American airman was being used as a pawn in the international game of diplomacy, and Jackson knew he had a greater chance of winning his release than any member of the Reagan Administration.

Jesse Jackson's relationship with the Arab world was a good one. He showed sympathy to the Palestinian cause despite vehement objections from the American Jewish community, and he had long-standing close ties to the Black Muslim movement in the United States, giving him a better understanding of the culture than most other Christian leaders. His opposition to American troops stationed in Lebanon also gave him a position of added trust with the Syrians.

But the final victory of Jesse Jackson in winning the release of Lt. Goodman did not lie in political maneuvering, or power politics; he traveled 8,000 miles to Syria to appeal on humanitarian grounds for the young American's release. He came quietly, not to accuse the Syrians, or even to berate his own President's failure, but to get the job done. "Whoever has the courage to act," he stated, "should act." Jesse Jackson had the courage to act while a nation held its breath in anticipation.

His chartered jet landed in Damascus under clear, starlit skies, the suspense mounting each day Jackson remained in Syria. He had traveled without a passport or official State Department sanction. His U.S. Secret Service protection was waived when he entered Syria, because Jackson wanted the Syrians to know he trusted them to protect him.

Finally he was allowed to meet and be photographed with Lt. Goodman, who reported good treatment from his captors.

Jackson postponed his departure date from Damascus, in hopes of a breakthrough in negotiations. Four days of rising tension passed until finally he was granted an audience with Syrian President Hafez Assad—rare for any Westerner. Reverend Jackson appealed directly to Assad to "break the cycle of pain" between his country and the United States. He urged Assad to make a humanitarian gesture of peace in the spirit of the Christmas holidays.

Jackson also argued his case on more pragmatic grounds, telling Assad he believed the continued imprisonment of Lt. Goodman was help ing the proponents of hawkish views back in the States. He suggested to the Syrian president that a failure to release Goodman might actually escalate the number of U.S. reconnaissance flights over Syrian-held territory.

Jesse Jackson's negotiations proved fruitful, as Goodman was released without ceremony from his Syrian prison and allowed to return with Jackson to the United States. The 27-year-old Navy airman and the black Presidential candidate flew back together on an Air Force jet, landing in the pre-dawn darkness at Andrews Air Force Base near Washington.

Jackson assessed his mission as "a giant step toward peace," and praised Assad's grant of freedom to Robert Goodman as a humanitarian gesture.

In White House ceremonies, President Reagan greeted the returning Navy airman as a hero, and shook hands with Reverend Jackson, calling his pilgrimage "a personal mission of mercy," and saying that Jackson had "earned our gratitude and our admiration."

They must have been bitter words for the President, because only days earlier, Reagan had snubbed Jesse Jackson prior to the Syrian trip, refusing to acknowledge Jackson's phone calls, and instructing the State Department to make their briefings as vague as possible. Jesse Jackson went to Syria with minimal support from his own government. Reagan's aides had no desire to see Jackson's mission succeed, and worried that a meeting with Reagan might lend credence to a mission they were sure would fail.

Jackson was successful in maneuvering Reagan into a defensive position before he left, since the President could hardly admit his desire for Jesse Jackson's failure. The fact that Lt. Goodman was black also added to the drama, and though Jackson never accused the President of racism in his failure to press for Goodman's release, this aspect was explored by the press. Just prior to leaving for Syria, Jackson released information which pointed out that Goodman's freedom had not even been discussed in the latest U.S.-Syrian negotiations. It was a damning piece of evidence against the Reagan Administration's handling of the affair, and may have been the final push Jackson needed to make his trip to Damascus.

But in the Rose Garden all was forgiven for the day devoted to celebrating Lt. Goodman's return. The crowds cheered, and Goodman's parents expressed their gratitude for Reverend Jackson's mission. The press covered the story extensively, and Jesse Jackson's prestige, as well as his standing in the polls, rose dramatically. He had proven himself a man of effective action as well as eloquent words. He had accomplished what neither his President nor the U.S. State Department could achieve, the peaceful, negotiated release of an American airman.

A speech at East Los Angeles College (located in a heavily Latino area) proved that Jackson's political appeal cut across racial and economic barriers.

Chapter 11

The Odyssey, Agony & Ecstasy

The Odyssey began as Reverend Jesse Jackson, country preacher turned politician, fired the boilers on the "freedom train" with the call—"Get on board! Get on board! But you got to be registered to ride."

"We can move from the slave ship to the championship!" urged Jackson. "From the guttermost to the uppermost! From the outhouse to the courthouse! From the statehouse to the White House!"

A voter's registration slip was the ticket to freedom, and people—once apathetic to the whole political process—rallied to Jackson's call, and urged in a single voice, to be echoed across the country, "Run, Jesse, run!

Run, Jesse, run! Run, Jesse, run!''

And he responded, announcing in November, 1983, "Mindful of the urgency of our times, I stand before you to acknowledge that, after deep reflection, the voice of duty has whispered, 'Thou must.' I rise to declare that 'I can.' ''

The Odyssey, powered by a Rainbow Coalition of blacks, Hispanics, women, gays, the poor, the aged, the handicapped and more—America's minorities, somehow chugged into the Democratic National Convention in San Francisco, where facing the agony of defeat, the Reverend Jesse Jackson delivered the speech that will be remembered along with Dr. Martin Luther King, Jr.'s historic "I Have A Dream Speech.''

He began slowly, celebrating the Democratic Party as "the best hope for redirecting our nation on a more humane, just and peaceful course.'' There was no trace of defeat in the rhythmic voice. Jackson was not a man who ran and fell. He finished in grand style, winning some 85% of the black vote and 20% of the white, against what had been considered insurmountable odds.

"This is not a perfect party,'' said Jackson. "We are not a perfect people. Yet we are called to a perfect mission: to feed the hungry; to clothe the naked; to house the homeless; to teach the illiterate; to provide jobs for the jobless; and to choose the human race over the nuclear race.''

He hadn't immediately won his audience. Jackson had learned patience over his years in the civil rights struggle, he had developed tenacity. He asked for a show of support, a "vote for a new direction for party . . . and

. . . nation; a vote for conscience and conviction.''

Jackson apologized, and the apology later gained more media attention than the demands he made of the party.

"If in my low moments," said Jackson, before the elite political body, "in word, deed or attitude, through some error of temper, taste or tone, I have caused anyone discomfort, created pain, or revived someone's fears . . . If there were occasion when my grape turned into a raisin and my joy bell lost its resonance . . . Charge it to my head, so limited in its finitude; not to my heart . . . I am not a perfect servant. I am a public servant . . . Be patient. God is not finished with me yet.''

Jackson called for a "revival of the spirit, inspired by a new vision and new possibilities." He urged them to "turn from finger pointing to clasped hands." And pressed them to "turn *to* each other and not *on* each other."

He spoke of the Rainbow Coalition that had brought him to the platform, and encouraged the expansion and unification of the Party.

He spoke to the continuing dangers of the Reagan Administration, cautioning, "In the final analysis we must be driven not by a negative—the fear of Reagan—but by the positive leadership and programs of the Democratic Party."

The world was stunned into respectful silence by the oratory of a man none figured to finish the race. Yet he had finished, and had the breath left to move them as a body, some to tears, not motivated by sympathy for a man who had won and lost, but by a need to celebrate a man who boasted that he could move mountains and proved that he could darn sure make them quake and tremble!!

Said this modern Hannibal, crusader for peace and justice: "no mountain is too high and no valley is too low; no forest is too dense, and no water is too deep—if your mind is made up."

Jackson ended in total command, and on a high note that brought the political "congregation" to its feet. "Suffering breeds character," said Jackson. "Character breeds faith. And in the end, faith will not disappoint. Faith, hope and dreams will prevail. We must be bound together by faith, sustained by hope and driven by a dream.

"Troubles won't last always. Our time has come. Our time has come. Our time has come. Thank you and God bless you."

The Jackson train left the Democratic Convention charged by the resounding declaration of hope and promise for the future.

On July 19, 1984, two days after he had transfixed those in attendance at the Democratic National Convention with his powerful oratory, the Rev. Jesse Jackson, a seasoned, weathered politician, was the country preacher again as he walked into his Thursday staff meeting, to address a select audience of volunteers and staff people.

"We cannot measure hope and renewed strength," Jackson said. "We cannot freeze these moments in time, we must assess them for what they are and let these moments go."

He smiled, sharing what, for him, was a moment of ecstasy as he said, "There's a difference between us having idle demonstrations about peace and making the peace movement mainline American politics ... we have brought the peace movement into the mainline thrust of politics in this country. I feel good about the fact that we broke some barriers demanding our rights to be human.''

Jackson recognized all who helped, all who made up the very alive Rainbow Coalition. ''We had disabled,'' he said, ''literally walking in their hearts as they rolled their chairs, because they really felt themselves being a part. In my judgment this represents the real victories for this campaign.'

And then it was time to close the meeting and for all to get on about the business the Jackson campaign had charged them with. There was much work to do—the work that has brought Reverend Jesse Jackson full force into the arena of American politics in the 1980s.

At the core of Jackson's power then and in his future plans was the ''Rainbow Coalition''—an organization that Jackson projected as representing America as it really is and Americans who had seldom been allowed a voice.

''Our flag is red, white and blue,'' Jackson had reminded the membership at the Democratic National Convention, ''but our nation is a rainbow—red, yellow, brown, black and white—and all are precious in God's sight. America is not like a blanket—one piece of unbroken cloth, the same color, the same texture, the same size. It is more like a quilt—many patches, many pieces, many colors and many sizes, all woven and held together by a common thread.''

The language was clear and precise, the images taken from the familiar. He spoke to and for the rejected, those tiny rivulets that trickled in the dry beds bordering the mainstream world, or were swallowed up and lost in cultural, political and economic anonymity.

Jesse Jackson, flanked by Secret Service security personnel, leaves the site of a May, 1988, speech in Los Angeles.